SELLING WITH AMAZON FBA

SELLING WITH AMAZON FBA: LEARN THE BEST STRATEGIES TO BUILD A $ 10,000/MONTH E-COMMERCE BUSINESS WITH AMAZON. SECRETS OF THE MOST SUCCESSFUL SELLERS ON AMAZON REVEALED.

Table of Contents

Description

If you're tired of working a nine-to-five job and are looking for an opportunity to start working for yourself from home, then you have probably looked into the concept of selling on Amazon. While you could sell on Amazon and handle all of your orders personally, taking advantage of Amazon's Fulfillment by Amazon program has many perks and benefits that allow you to grow your business faster and reach higher profit margins than doing it alone.

Of those perks, the most desirable one is that Amazon can handle all of the time-consuming work of packaging and shipping your goods to buyers, along with customer service and handling returns. This allows you more time to focus on finding great products that people will want to buy, and ultimately, more time to do the things you truly love to do.

Of course, for those with money to invest or a product already lined up, the same steps can be applied to create your new income stream on the fast track. For those that want to expand past the introductory method of selling what you already have, we will also discuss the various ways to source new products, expand your inventory, and get the most out of your experience as a seller that utilizes this great service from Amazon.

This guide will focus on the following:

- Set up amazon FBA
- Branding your product & making it stand out
- Creating your product listing
- Amazon FBA and tax season
- Tools that you will need to get started
- How to sell your product?
- Understanding amazon's success
- Quality control
- Mistakes to avoid... AND MORE!!!

Introduction

Amazon is perhaps the most competitive marketplace on the planet. It is a place where more than 2,000,000 merchants fight over 400,000,000 customers. The competition is extremely fierce, considering they have to go against each other and the platform itself. However, there are many resellers who stand as living proof of the success that they have achieved on this channel. Most of them are using a very interesting service provided on this platform called Fulfillment by Amazon. The platform favors the users of this service because of two different reasons. The first one is to make money (obviously). The second one is to help other sellers to have stellar delivery standards. After all, the Amazon shoppers deserve such level of standards when it comes to delivery and customer service. Some of the main perks provided by the FBA option include:

1. Eligibility for free delivery for the Prime members

In plenty of cases, the FBA products are associated with the Prime logo, which sends a strong message to the shopper: the product can be shipped for free within 48 hours, and there are benefits that come with this subscription. Just in the US, there are more than 100,000,000 Prime members; that's why they are known as Amazon's big spenders and loyal shoppers. FBA products are exposed to this group, which offers the FBA merchant a great advantage over the others.

2. Amazon Coupons and Free Shipping

It is apparent that Amazon offers free shipping for products above $25 (regardless if the shopper is a Prime member or not). However, the truth is that most of the FBA products are already in this category. It's also the same when it comes to the Amazon coupons, in which case the FBA goods automatically qualify. They are, by definition, eligible products and, as mentioned in the description of free shipping, this service is applicable for them.

3. Better Rankings

FBA is a criteria that is taken into consideration by Amazon's A9 algorithm. This means that such goods are favored when listing the results, as well as getting better rankings and more sales. Every time Amazon displays results for a search term, the first two pages are the only ones with FBA products. The rest of the pages may not even matter for the average shopper on this platform.

4. Seriously Increased Chances of Getting Buy Box

The Buy Box option is the one that every merchant dream of getting because it promises the best placement on Amazon. This function enables easier sales of a specific product. FBA products have the highest priority in this case.

5. Trusted by Amazon

There is no better certificate for a merchant on the Amazon platform than its seal of approval. It's like a certificate of excellence, a proof that this merchant sells the best quality products and takes special care of their customers.

When it comes to shipping, FBA is the best option if you sell massively on Amazon or it is your main selling channel. The company puts its expertise on the table since the merchant using FBA will benefit from discounted carrier services, as well as professional customer support service related to product tracking, or returns. This is how you can benefit from top-notch services provided by Amazon. However, before rushing in to sign up for FBA, you need to know the costs first because this service doesn't come free of charge. There are fulfillment costs, storage fees (depending on the period your inventory sits in Amazon's warehouse), along with the amount that you need to pay for every sale. Not to mention that, in order to succeed and be at least one step ahead of your competitors, you have to seriously consider advertising as an option to boost rankings and sales (conversions).

Product sourcing is very important when you have to stay competitive, considering finding a supplier that can deliver high-quality and reasonably-priced products is a must. You can get a vague idea of the profit margin when you know the estimated price for which you will sell your products. If you have a merchandise that you know will sell and is not sold by many, you can do the math (estimate all the costs) and decide whether it is worth to go ahead with FBA.

If you decide to embark on the journey to win tons of money by selling on Amazon, then the FBA is definitely the right option to select. However, you can't hope to get high sales if your content is poor. You will need to optimize it, use keywords naturally, structure your product description very well, and include the key features of the product in there. Also, make sure to use high-quality pictures before launching your merchandise. Once you have the first sale, you will already notice that your rank is improving significantly, but you also have to pay attention to reviews to get as many as you can and take them into consideration to improve the quality of your products or provided services. Reviews are the most influential statements for any consumers since they can convert a simple view into sales. Everyone is on Amazon to sell; hence, the more you sell, the better. This should be the main objective for any merchant.

If you take all of the above into consideration, your chances of succeeding will increase significantly. Although this is a very competitive environment, there is no better place to sell products than Amazon. This is the place to be. A large of volume of sales is within your grasp, and it's only up to you to decide how much you want to sell and how visible you want to be to your potential customers. The only thing left to say is: Good luck!

Chapter 1 Foundations of FBA

Fulfillment by Amazon is all about strategizing; the difference between selling as a merchant and selling as a professional with FBA is the amount of time you will have to devote to maximizing your potential profit. Here are some basic guiding principles you will need to be aware of:

Buy Low, Sell High

This is how you earn money as an Amazon seller. There are multiple ways to do this; you can use the stores around you as a local resource for purchasing items cheaply. Depending on where you live, you may even be able to make money off of products that are not available elsewhere, and buyers are willing to pay big money simply for access. You may find yourself buying items at their normal price and selling them for a profit. This will be essential to running your business.

Competition

As an Amazon seller, your competition on the marketplace is huge. You must strive to be the best, most efficient seller you can be; this will lead to better reviews, which leads to higher listings. Amazon is a perfect platform for breeding competition among its vendors. It is set up in such a way to advantage the sellers who are already doing well.

This means to make the most of your business, you will need to run a tight ship, constantly checking to be sure you are offering the most competitive pricing. As you start off, you will need to focus on building credibility among your buyers and improving your reputation so you can move higher up in the ranks. There are strategies you can use to increase your visibility that will be addressed in this guide.

Technology

With Amazon FBA, you will be at your optimal productivity by using technology such as your cellphone to stay current with the top-trending products and to take advantage of the most complex apps on the market to calculate your best chances with selling.

Selling on Amazon FBA requires a level of dedication to working on a computer that those uncomfortable with the idea of adapting to new technology will be wary of. You will need to stay in tune and on top of the latest trends in online marketing if you wish to have a chance against the competition. This guide will direct you to some of the best resources on the market for getting the most out of your business.

What direction will this take you?

There are two ways to sell through Amazon FBA: through retail arbitrage, and with private labeling. People run immensely profitable businesses with both approaches, but they require different commitments.

Each form requires significant investment of time. With proper handling, you can turn your Amazon business into a full-time source of income. It doesn't happen overnight, however, and it takes time to build up the reputation and customer base to turn a sustained and secure source of income. This guide will equip you with the tools to understand the ways of the market, starting with the basics of Fulfillment and moving into the more complex routes, such as private labeling, toward the end.

Create your Account

First things first: you have to have an Amazon Seller account. If you are already selling on Amazon, you just need to register your account and "add FBA to your account." Otherwise, you will need an Amazon Seller Account. Sign up by scrolling to the links at the bottom of the Amazon homepage. Under the Header "Make Money with Us," click on the hyperlink that reads "Sell on Amazon." From there, you can register directly as an FBA seller, or start with your individual seller account.

Depending on what you sell, you may want to start with the individual seller before moving up to a professional seller account. There are advantages to starting with a professional seller account. Professional sellers are able to sell items that are restricted from individual sellers. Professional seller accounts are free for the first Month, after which you can renew your subscription for a fee.

Individual sellers are sellers that ship less than 40 items per month. If you are planning to sell more than that, it is advisable to go for the professional account. There are differences in the fees you are charged as a seller depending on which account you use, which are explained in a later section. You can always upgrade from an individual account to a seller account – however, the opportunity for the first free month of selling professionally is only available when you first sign up. If you know you are serious about Amazon FBA as an investment in your future, go for the professional account and receive the first month free. You could always cancel it before the next month's charges set in.

All you need to sign up is your credit card information, name, address, a professional-sounding and snappy display name, and information to verify your identity.

In order to sell, you must complete a participation agreement that obligates you to fulfill Amazon's terms and conditions for selling. There are guidelines you will need to follow to be eligible to sell and restrictions on what you can and cannot sell. A partial list of guidelines is included in this guide, but be sure to check the Amazon official website for up-to-date information.

Now that you are registered to sell, you must figure out how you will acquire the products you will be shipping. There are many ways to do this, but this book will cover two main methods: arbitrage and private-labeling. Since arbitrage is the main way people usually get started, we will cover that method first for the foundations. Private labeling will be addressed in later sections.

Arbitrage

This is the word used to describe one of the fastest ways to get involved in Amazon FBA. There are multiple forms of arbitrage: be it through retail, garage sales, or online. It is the process of buying items at a discount or on clearance and selling them for a higher price through Amazon

Scanning and Scouting

Scanning and scouting is the most common way to begin your venture in retail arbitrage. Key to retail arbitrage are the apps you will use to scan your products and figure out the likelihood of selling off the items in the store. This business is not about taking chances; there are apps available for calculating the approximate profit you stand to make from selling such an item.

The Amazon Seller app is available for Android and iOS phones. Inventory Lab is another service that some recommend as it offers other tools for increasing your efficiency as well. Other scanning apps, such as Scoutify, Barcode Booty, and Profit Bandit, require a fee but come highly recommended.

In retail arbitrage, you scan the barcode on the product in the clearance aisle of the store. The app will display the information you need to determine how good of a deal it is and how much you are likely to earn selling that item. It calculates the profit for you. Depending on the app, you will also be asked to input the cost associated with your selling of the item – for example, the cost of the shipping materials you will need to send it to Amazon. This cost is one you will need to figure out over a period of time, because it is highly dependent on your personal circumstances.

You can repeat this process with retail items in any store, as well as with products of sale at discounts online and at garage sales. This can be done without an app, but it is easier to use your phone than to write the prices down and checking it at home. In the end, it is a personal preference, and trying both ways to see which is more efficient time-wise will not hurt.

The biggest issue people have with retail arbitrage is the amount of time that one must spend traveling from store to store. It requires a lot of energy. With proper scanning, however, it can pay off. It is generally wise to avoid items that are not less than 50% marked down in price. The best deals are on clearance for over 70% if you can manage it.

This type of arbitrage can be applied at yard sales or discount retailers, particularly with items like books. You will not necessarily be "scanning" if you look up pricing on items online, but the principle remains the same.

Scanning for the First Time

One way to feel comfortable and test out your Amazon FBA account is to scan products around your household that have not yet been removed from the packaging. This will give you an idea of how the apps work so you will be more comfortable when you are in an actual store scanning products. Furthermore, you can capitalize on the profitable opportunities you have lying around at home! Take a trip into the basement and make use of all those unwanted Christmas gifts. You may even go so far as to offer to help cleaning out your relatives' closets. You will be surprised at the rankings some products reach!

It is important to be aware of the restrictions on selling some products. Products with restrictions on them will be labeled as such on the scanning apps, but it is worth digging around the guidelines established by Amazon to know what you are getting into. A later section of this book addresses the very basics of what can and cannot be sold through Amazon, but for this type of information, it is best to go to the source.

With Amazon Doing All the Work, What *Does* the Seller Do?

With Amazon doing all the heavy lifting, what do you do as the seller? Procure the goods and find your suppliers for one thing, which is possibly the most important part of the job. Without the right products and a reliable supplier, there will be no business, to begin with. You have other tasks as a seller (which Amazon will not do for you), include:

- *Keeping Track of Your Inventory* - Managing your inventory is going to be your responsibility. Amazon will notify you when your inventory is running low. It is your job to make sure that the items you sell are always in stock.

- *Marketing Your Products* - Amazon does all the backend work for you so you can focus on the more interesting aspects of the business. Like marketing and promoting your products. Competition is high in the online retail space and you need to put your product in the spotlight and make it visible to people who want your products. Starting a store alone is not going to be enough to drive sales that are going to require some effort on your part.

- *Pay Amazon* - Excellent service comes at a price of course. You will have to pay Amazon the necessary fees for using its storage and fulfillment facilities. However, given the kind of service you can expect from Amazon, fees are well worth it.

With Amazon doing all the time-consuming work for you on your behalf (including storage, order fulfillment, handling the delivery and returns and dealing with the customer service side of your business), the fees you're paying for is essentially for the stellar customer service, which is available around the clock and for reliable shipping and access to the most advanced and largest fulfilment networks in this world.

When it comes to reputation, reliability and top-notch service, Amazon is at the top of its game. Not many e-Commerce retailers are able to match entirely what this giant can do (it is the best in the business for a reason). This contributes to a big part of its success and if you are willing to pay the reasonable fees required, you can be a part of that success too.

Chapter 2 Skills Needed for Amazon FBA

At this point, your Amazon Seller Central account is launched and you are serious about starting your business. You have made the commitment, and you are ready to get started so that you can start seeing profits come through on the commitment that you have made. Before we really get started, however, I want to get clear on some skills that you are going to need, in order to launch your Amazon FBA and make a passive income through your efforts.

Every single business requires a unique skill set that is going to help you earn an income with that business, and Amazon FBA is no different. Although this platform does not require nearly as many skills for you to succeed, it does require you to have some degree of skills so you should be prepared to understand what these skills are, and continually invest in them in order to generate success.

Building Your Competitive Edge

Although building your competitive edge is a strategy, it can also be considered a skill, as you do grow better at identifying, building, and honing your competitive edge over time. Some people seem to have the strength right off the bat and can identify what helps them stay competitive against the rest of the crowd, and then leverage that competitive edge to succeed right from day one. This is often the case when you identify stories of people who started making tens of thousands, hundreds of thousands, or even millions within their first year of business.

Even if you are not particularly knowledgeable or skilled in this area at first, you can certainly build your skill at being a competitive business owner. The key to identifying and growing your competitive edge knows what makes you more desirable over any other business in your niche. For example, Lulu Lemon is an athletic clothing company based out of Vancouver, British Columbia and it uses its competitive edge of being a local company with high-quality clothes to market to its customers. Apple is a well-known technology company that has the competitive edge of having products that are sleek and that have a modern or futuristic design to them, which they use to appeal to their customers with. Every company that has ever generated any level of success has identified its competitive edge, and then made virtually every single decision in their company based on how they can leverage their competitive edge to maximize their success.

When it comes to being a more competitive business owner as a skill, you will find that the more that you think with the mindset of "what is my competitive edge and how can I leverage it?", the more it comes naturally for you to find these competitive opportunities. As a result, it will become easier for you to create that competitive edge even further and leverage it even more for your business.

Branding Your Business

Much like with finding and leveraging your competitive edge, branding your business is both a strategy and a skill that you have to develop over time. On the issue of seeing your brand as a skill, the easiest way to understand why it is a skill is to recognize that your brand is an identity with its own personality. Even if your brand is based on you, it is going to have its own image, tone of voice, and other elements of it that are based on its own personality rather than yours.

To help you build your skill in branding, you can spend as much time as possible getting to know your brand and to understand what it looks like and who it is. Get to know your brand as if you were getting to know a new friend, and put just as much effort into understanding everything from the more obvious surface-level elements of your brand to the deeper and more meaningful elements of your brand. For example, you might already have a decent comprehension of the fact that your brand is represented by yellow and teal and that you use Arial font types with it, and you might know that it has a more playful and fun tone of voice to it. However, do you know exactly what words your brand would use to speak with your audience in order to share a relatable and impactful message with them? Do you know how and where your brand would incorporate yellow and teal into its imagery to create an image that is not only identifiable but also enjoyable to look at? Do you know how your brand would communicate with customers in private messages to create a professional conversation that still held the tone of your brand?

Knowing these nuances helps you really understand the brand that you are portraying and how you can leverage it to connect with other people. It might take time for you to get to know your brand on this level, but eventually, you will find that the image captions or product descriptions that once took you hours to come up with, eventually only take a few minutes. This is because you can effectively "get into character" as your brand and portray your brand in the best way possible, while still leveraging it to earn sales from your customers.

Tracking and Monitoring Analytics

Your analytics are an important asset to your business as they directly tell you what your customers think about the way that you are doing business. For the most part, your customers are probably not going to go out of their way to message you with feedback on how they feel about your new products, or what they think about your latest marketing techniques, which is why analytics matter. Analytics give you the opportunity to identify what marketing materials are working, which products are the most popular, and what is ultimately causing your customers to purchase from you, or not purchase from you if you are seeing a rut in your sales.

When considering analytics, you are going to need to know how to monitor your analytics directly on Amazon FBA, as they are directly linked to your shoppers and visitors. However, you are also going to want to apply the same skills to your social media marketing strategies, in order to see how your marketing strategies are developing, too. This way, you can feel confident that both your marketing efforts and your shop are performing to the best of their ability, giving you the best chances at earning a sale in your business.

Expense Tracking and Monitoring

In addition to monitoring and tracking your analytics, you also want to monitor and track your expenses related to your business. When you first launch a business, it can be easy to get lost in all of the various purchases that you make to get your business off the ground and get it in front of your audience. From your Amazon Seller Central account fees to advertising fees and product-related fees, your expenses can rack up quickly, and if you are not careful, they can take a toll on your business.

Naturally, when you first launch a business you are going to go into the negatives for a while, as you are going to be spending your own cash on these early purchases. At that point, you will not have any sales, so you will not have made enough profits to make up for the money that you are spending on launching your business. For that reason, you want to be modest in the way that you spend money early on, so that you can quickly earn some revenue and pay back the expenses that you put into launching your business. The sooner that you can break even, the better, as this means you are not out on your own expenses to launch your business.

Just because you want to be modest with your expenses, however, does not mean that you want to be cheap in the way that you are spending your expenses. The idea instead is to consider what expenses are necessary and then purchase the best quality of each product or service that you can reasonably afford. This way, you have a great brand to launch with and you can always upgrade or add more expenses or features later.

After you have launched your business, you are still going to need to pay attention to your expenses and track them effectively. You need to make sure that you are always working toward staying profitable and that you are never spending more than you have or more than you have to, in order to operate your business. Keep your expenses as low as you reasonably can, while still running a quality business, so that you are able to run a great business while also earning an excellent profit.

Investing in Your Marketing Skills

When it comes to Amazon FBA, aside from sourcing and purchasing product and then having them shipped to Amazon, your only other role is to market. With the right marketing skills in place, you can drive huge amounts of traffic to your website and get your products seen. This way, you have higher chances of actually having people purchase your products, which is exactly how you earn your revenue in your business.

As you continue to run your business, you should also continue to work on learning how to grow your marketing skills. Do not be afraid to invest in marketing courses, to take seminars or other learning sessions that can help you learn, and to read about the latest in marketing strategies online. The more that you can keep yourself up to date with how to market, as well as the latest trends in marketing, the more you are going to be able to launch your business with great success.

Eventually, the more successful you grow with marketing the easier it will be for you to get your products in front of customers. This way, you will have an even easier time selling your products because you will be doing and saying all of the right things to get the attention of your audience and to encourage them to look at your shop and possibly purchase your products. Again, the better you get with this, the easier it will be for you to do and the more fluidly you will find yourself earning greater momentum off of each post you make or product you launch.

Chapter 3 Do Product Ideas Grow from Trees?

The building block and foundation of this business that everything else will rest upon is the product(s) and *ultimately* the niche you decide to enter into. Pick the correct one and you've got a niche that can provide a sustainable and steady income for a long time to come; choose a bad one and you're going to be paying Amazon so you can rent space in their warehouse. What we are referring to as niche in this case is the market or industry you decide to enter into, generally you will want to start from a narrow point then expand out. So instead of workout gear, you target a certain niche within that wide market such as yoga gear, running gear, gym gear, or whatever other sub-niche there is inside of workout gear.

Selling products on Amazon follows the same rules as any product that is to be sold to the general public: you need to have demand; you need to target a specific market or customer (not just selling boots, but perhaps more specifically Texas leather boots); and you need a product that can easily be found that stands out from competitors.

Before we get into all of the above though, let's figure out what the heck you're actually going to sell. Well, it's best for you to sell what you want to sell, so what is it that you would like to sell?

Haha, we're not going to leave you in the headlights like that! In descending order of easiest to most 'difficult' ways to finding what product or niche to sell in, this is what we recommend you do:

1. Figure out what your interests, hobbies, and passions are and write down a list of them. Now figure out what items are used or related to these interests, hobbies, or passions. Anything you have great interest or really like doing is a great place to start. Think about the things you do when you procrastinate or the things you daydream or think about a lot.

2. Write a touch list for the next 24 hours. Anything you physically touch or interact with over the next 24 hours; make a long list of all of these items either on paper or on your phone. You can also ask friends or family to do this for you too and to pass the list on to you.

3. Look through your bank and credit card statements and make a list of things you've bought that you could potentially sell. It also helps to consider any products or areas you've found yourself or others frustrated with in terms lack of choice, functionality, pricing or otherwise as there is the potential to fill that void in the market for that product.

4. When watching TV you can get ideas from shows, shopping channels, or late night infomercials. Another good way to get ideas is to sign up to blogs, online

magazines or newsletters (email or physical) in certain industries and scour through them when they send you their latest editions.

5. Visit online stores and drill through their categories: Amazon, eBay, Pinterest, Etsy, Alibaba, DH-Gate, Ali-Express, Global-Sources are a few to start with. Make a list of products that you would be interested in selling. Make sure to look at similar or frequently bought items if the websites provide suggestions and also check out the Best Seller lists as they prove the product is already in demand (be careful here as the demand in certain categories can be so low that a product selling 30 products a month could still be tagged as a best seller)

6. Hit up Google and type in the search field the following (with the quotation marks in the same spot): "Amazon Best Sellers Rank: #number in category" site:amazon.com. So for #number you would put #500 or whatever best seller rank you are targeting and in the category put the name of any category or subcategory you're interested in selling in (i.e. "Amazon Best Sellers Rank: #540 in Sports & Outdoors" site:amazon.com. This will show you the product that is currently ranked at the best seller rank you input in Google on Amazon for the category you selected (generally the product will have changed ranks as Google is slightly delayed), and from there you can visit the product page and see what the product is. You can also check out the items that are

frequently bought or similar to the product, or if the product/niche isn't to your fancy, go back to Google and keep changing the best seller rank or categories to get new product ideas.

7. (Advanced) Visit product fairs such as HKTDC, Global-Sources, or Canton Fair and see the products and get to know the suppliers on a face-to-face basis. This is a bit more of an advanced option as it helps to know what type of products to look out for and have the ability to quickly check the viability of certain products whilst you're at the fairs. How-ever if you live closely to where any of these Fairs are held (Hong Kong and China mainly) or you're simply passing by when they're on, there's nothing holding you back from checking it out! You'll be guaranteed to have hundreds of product ideas swarming in your head afterwards.

To elaborate a little further on option 1 above. What are things you enjoy doing, or what are things you find yourself doing on a regular basis? For all of these activities consider any items that you use, bring along with you, or that are remotely related to these activities or events. It helps a ton further down the track if you can pick a product or niche from this option, especially when you start looking at building a brand around the product or niche.

Why is this the case? Because you know the target market on an intimate level, how is that? Because you are that target market, you are an "avatar" (ideal customer) for the market as long as you can find a product to private label that you would WANT to personally buy, then you can easily market the product and create a brand around it. It will also be easier for you to differentiate the product so that it stands out from competitor's products but more on that later. By taking this option you can leverage what you already know and have experience in and this saves you time and resources later down the track. Marketing efforts will be halved because you don't have to think about what would trigger your customers to buy your products over competitors, you already know what will accomplish that.

Stop - It's Hammer TIME!

Hold off from the above for a second! This is the only time you'll ever hear that around here so we suggest you embrace it. You can save a ton of time if you have a basic understanding of what type of products and niches you should be looking out for to begin with.

Firstly as we've already specified, you will want to look at picking a product you can build a brand around. What's the difference between a product and a brand? Well a product is one passive income stream, a brand represents a business. A brand in this case is Nike, UnderArmour, McDonalds, Coca Cola, and so forth. Okay so how do we build and make a brand? Well you create your own logo (hence private label) with your brand name and work towards selling more than one product in the future. This includes variations to your product. What we mean here is that if you sell stools, there can be many products and variations to a stool, there can be a sitting or standing stool, high or low stool etc, all of these are different products yet are only slightly different. Why build a brand instead of just selling a lot of products individually? Simply put, it's much more sustainable over the long term and arguably results in more profit for the effort and time put in by you. You will want to build a brand that stands out in your market and niche so when people think of you, they think of your products. So if we're trying to dominate the stool market and our brand name is "Three Stoolers" (homage to the three stooges) and there are 5, 10, or more products under this brand, prospective customers can see this and may associate a sense of credibility to products sold under this brand as having more than one product shows that this brand or company has experience selling stools.

The benefits of building a brand far outweigh the costs in terms of resource, time, and effort. As you build a brand you are products are perceived as being more trustworthy and reputable, you will be able to start selling on your own without the help of Amazon (so you begin to run the show the whole way from receiving customers to getting them the end product), you can dominate a niche or market thorough this means capturing more sales and so forth. Eventually you will want to venture into building a blog or website, setting up social media channels however that is a long way away. It's good to keep this in mind though and it's why we have stressed it's a lot easier and smarter to pick a niche or product that you have a passion or interest in, especially when you'll be spending time in this niche 5 or 10 years in the future. As mentioned before however, you don't need to pick a niche that you have a genuine interest in, it only means you'll need to dedicate time and effort towards learning about your target market and the products you're selling or perhaps outsourcing this and paying others to do the legwork for you such as writing content for your blog, website, and social media.

The Winning Factors

Before forming your list of product and niche ideas, keep these factors at the forefront of your mind and it will help you cull down on your initial product idea list. If you'd prefer to just note everything down then cut the list down later that's perfectly fine. Please keep in mind that these are merely guidelines to follow and don't need to be adhered to 100%! If the product satisfies the majority of the factors but misses a few here and there but is still profitable it would be silly not to go for it. You can always estimate the shipping fees or revenue based on the dimensions of your product and units sold per month, it's also possible to have a quick glance at what the cost per unit will be for the product from potential suppliers by checking Alibaba, or Global-Sources. Also if you keep in mind that other sellers will also be following a similar criteria for picking a product, this limits many sellers to the same pool of products and thus stepping outside of this pool can result in less competition and untapped profits. It pays a lot in this business to not follow the crowd and go where the path is less travelled. For now though it's highly recommended you stick to the factors below as best you can for your first product so you can get the ball rolling and gain some experience before you even consider taking any risks. So without further ado, the factors to consider are listed below.

Physical Characteristic Factors

1. Is the product small?

A product less than 18 inches in length (on the longest side) is considered standard sized and anything greater than this will be classed as an oversized product on Amazon. Oversized products result in greater shipping, handling, and storage fees which in turn mean a lower profit margin. Other factors to satisfy a standard sized product are 14 inches or less on the median side and 8 inches or less on the shortest side with the product not weighing more than 20 pounds (roughly 9 kgs). Once a product is classed as oversized you can only store 500 units in Amazon's warehouses to begin with however this can be increased over time if your products are selling. A quick and easy test for this factor is to ask yourself if the product will fit inside of a shoebox, it's generally fine if it's slightly larger than one too.

2. Is the product lightweight?

It's best to go with a product that is as light as possible, anything less than 5 pounds (2.25kg) would be most ideal. The lighter the better for the most part as it simply means lower shipping costs and fees. When it comes to shipping it comes down to weight and volume so it's better to satisfy small and lightweight as opposed to large and lightweight or small and heavy. You can get a rough estimate for what a product will weigh by looking at similar products on Amazon as they will have their weight listed, or you can check the weight of products based off what manufacturers' state on sourcing websites. You will want to clarify the weight of the product directly with manufacturers before engaging with them

3. Is the product simple?

When you're starting out it's advised to avoid electronics as they have a higher risk of failing and more complexity when sourcing products from manufacturers. Apart from this you'll want to aim for products that don't have parts that break easily during shipping and handling such as glass. Having a lot of moving mechanical parts on a product can also be a risk as there's the potential for these parts to break off. From a long term perspective if any of these three issues ever occurred for a product it would not be a pretty sight as your listing would more than likely have a lot of returns coming back as well as negative reviews, and if you offer warranty you can bet a lot of claims would be coming in. The last thing to consider in this scenario is how dangerous the product could potentially be, say for example with hover-boards that caught on fire in recent times, or knives just because of the nature of them. Try to avoid anything that could result in a potential law suit.

4. *Can the product be private labeled and modified or improved?* We want to choose products that can be private labeled and by this we mean manufacturers actually manufacture the product and also to ensure you aren't competing against major name brands on a product. For example, Huggies are known for diapers, you wouldn't necessarily want to compete against them as they dominate such a big share of the market. So it's best to avoid products that have one or two well-known major brands that dominate the market.

By modified or improved we're referring to a product that has the potential to be differentiated from competition in the market in some manner by making slight alterations to the product during the manufacturing phase. This could be something as simple as changing a screwing feature on a product to flip open instead. You can easily find these points of differentiations when researching competitors by looking at their reviews 3 stars and below. Avoid the "me too" products, there's not much point going into a market and offering the same exact product as 5 other competitors as it only makes it harder to stand out. Sometimes you can't help it and you have to go for the "me too" product but if you do, make sure your product stands out in some other way (photos, bullet/description, title, etc.) Go for a product you can differentiate or improve on as it will be better for your brand in the long term and it'll make it easier for you to market and sell your product.

One common way of differentiating a product is through bundling, either selling the product in pairs, threes, fours, or fives, or bundling the product with another related product such as a yoga mat and yoga towel.

5. Can you build a brand around the product/niche and also sell more related products around it?

Hopefully this has been hammered into you enough by now but we're here to build a brand which is a business, not simply sell one product and retire on the beaches of Cabo as that's difficult to do. What we mean by this is that you should do some quick preliminary research on similar items and check how well they are selling. There are a few methods for this such as using Google Keyword Planner or just looking at frequently bought together or similar items on competitor's product pages. An example of this is dog nail clippers and dog hair trimmers, they're related and they can be leveraged for you to cross-promote the products between your customers when you release your second product under the brand. Furthermore you can branch out to other pet items under the brand by selling similar products for birds and cats. A quick trick to helping you identify similar products you can sell is just going on to Amazon and finding sellers who sell the product you intend to, click to their Seller Store page (click on their seller name on the product page) and you can see all the products that they are selling and get an idea of what's possible.

6. *(OPTIONAL FACTOR) Is the product a little weird, odd, or unsexy?*

7. No one really wants to sell unique and weird items. A good test to see if a product satisfies this factor is considering how your friends, family, or colleagues would respond if you told them you wanted to sell this product. If they think it's cool or a great idea than it's possible other people have already thought of it or will think of it in the future and hence there's likely to be more competition. If they will think of you oddly or weirdly, jackpot! This is an optional factor to consider because we'll be looking at assessing our competition anyway during our research phase however it's more likely than not this factor will result in less competition in the future. In this business, you will want to steer away from where everyone else is going into and be the first to find new land so you have first mover's advantage.

Market Research Factors

These factors deal more with the market rather than the product itself. This research will be primarily conducted on Amazon.

7. Is there enough demand in the market to sell at least 10 units a day?

To determine this you will be using the Best Seller Rank on Amazon for products as a guide. Keep in mind we will want to have a good amount of units being sold in a month for the product, we generally refer to this as the depth of the market. More on this later.

For now we'll do a quick primer as to how the Best Seller Rank works on Amazon. For each major category such as Home & Kitchen, Sports & Outdoors, Toys & Games and so on, they have ALL of the items under the category that are listed on Amazon assigned a best seller rank within that category. How this best seller rank is determined is based on how many sales the product has made and this is updated hourly. So each product under the major category is ranked in the order based on how many sales they have made, so the product with rank of #546 has sold more units than #547 in the category of Home & Kitchen or whatever major category they are in. For this reason, the sales rank number for each category indicates a different number of estimated units sold because the total number of products that are bought in Sports & Outdoors could be less than the total products bought in Home & Kitchen.

8. What price range will the product sell for and will you be able to make $10 profit on each product sold?

If you can sell 10 units a day and earn $10 profit on each unit you'll make at least $3000 profit a month on the product. To estimate what the price range for a product would be just ask yourself how much you'd be willing to pay for it or visit Amazon and see what price the product is being sold for. Look for products in the price range of $15 to $50, anything lower than

$15 and shipping fees are more than likely to eat the majority of the profits unless it is a really lightweight and small product. $50 has been set as the upper limit because this is roughly the upper end of where impulse purchase are made. Above $50 and people are a bit more reluctant to buying a product straight off the bat without doing some research into alternative options or the reputation of the company selling the product.

9. How tough is the competition?

How many reviews do your competitors have? Is the market dominated by thousands of reviews and big name brands in the top six spots? How well optimized are your competitor's product listings?

Chapter 4 Placing Your Order

In this section I will be covering how your make the first order for your products with your chosen supplier. You will need to setup an account to begin the ordering process - here are the factors to consider:

Forms: As part of the ordering process, you will generally need to fill in some basic forms. Some suppliers may want to see a reseller's license but this is pretty rare.

Payment Method: You will typically need to make a payment up front, however many suppliers will allow a small down payment if requested. I usually pay a down payment of 1/3, and then complete the final 2/3 of payment before shipment. You will also need to figure out the payment methods that they accept: Wire, PayPal, credit/debit card. I usually use Western Union but there are fees associated with this.

Getting design plans: Some suppliers can do your designs for you, but you can send over files that your designers have created. Find out the specifications for what they require, e.g. file types, image sizes etc.

Making your down payment: Most reputable suppliers will accept a down payment which is a percentage of the total cost. If they do not, I would be skeptical about their legitimacy. You can then pay the remaining payment once your products have been manufactured. I recommend getting pictures continuously to make sure your products are actually being manufactured and shipped out.

Waiting for your product to be made: Whilst you are waiting for your products to be made, you should start making your Amazon product listing page which is covered in the following sections of the book.

Giving your supplier your FBA information: Before your manufacture ships out your products, they will need to include am Amazon packing and label slip which allows them to be correctly sent to an Amazon fulfillment center. Amazon provides these and you can simply email these to your supplier.

Detailed Shipping Details
FBA Labeling: When your products are in the Amazon warehouse, they will require a 'FNSKU' label. You can get your supplier to do this, but for ease and efficiency I strongly recommend letting Amazon do this for you for a cost of $0.20 per unit.

If you have any issues with labeling, don't hesitate to contact Amazon Seller Support. In my experience, they have been excellent and very thorough with guiding me through the labeling process. They will even stay on the phone and walk you through the required steps.

Having your products inspected: It is usually a good idea to have your products inspected when making your first order. These can be done by a 3rd party, but I recommend having the products sent directly to you so you can inspect the quality of the products and then have these forwarded to the Amazon fulfillment center. This will ensure you don't sell any products that have significant issues which will hugely impact your brand and chances of doing well on Amazon.

Action Checklist

Below is a checklist of actions from the last few sections that you must complete before moving on to the next steps:

- Create a list of 5 suppliers for your top 5 preferred products
- Contact each supplier and ask the questions as previously covered.
- Select the final product to go for.
- Order at least 2 samples for this product from different suppliers.
- Narrow down and choose your main supplier.
- Place your order with the supplier and make your initial down payment.
- Obtain relevant shipping labels from Amazon and send these to your supplier.
- Make the final payment and have your products shipped!

Chapter 5 Set Up Amazon FBA

The first step, as you know, is to set up an account with Amazon FBA. Creating your account is the first step because this is where you are going to gain access to everything that you need to launch your Amazon FBA business. With your Amazon account in place, you will have the main hub for your Amazon FBA business fixed in place, so that you are ready to begin selling on Amazon.

What You Need to Know About Amazon Seller Central Account

Your Amazon Seller Central account is the foundation for everything that you do in your business, as you cannot do anything without this account. Although you could complete this step later on after you have already built the rest of your business out, it might not be a great idea, as this will prevent you from acquainting yourself with the platform and learning to navigate it beforehand. Building your account in advance gives you the opportunity to understand none of the features available to you ahead of time, so when considering the time to launch you is attempting to understand a new platform, in addition to managing a launch. As well, many people find that creating the actual account makes their business feel a lot more real, and helps them stay committed to seeing their decision to launch an Amazon FBA business through in a timely fashion.

Amazon Seller Central is going to give you access to everything that you need to know about your Amazon FBA business. Here, you are going to be able to introduce and design your storefront, manage product listings, oversee customer service inquiries, manage your revenue, and gain access to important information such as when stock needs to be reordered and where to send it to. In your account, you will find options to reorder stock and register that stock with Amazon so that they can actually receive your inventory, which is crucial.

Essentially, everything that you will ever need to do regarding the creation, maintenance, or running of your business is going to involve the Amazon Seller Central account in one way or another. The more you can grow comfortable with the platform now, in advance, the easier it is going to be for you to rely on this platform and use it to run your business.

Creating Your Amazon FBA Account

Creating an Amazon FBA account is simple, and does not take more than a few minutes. You will start by going to Amazon's website and scrolling down to the very bottom of the page so that you can see their footer navigation bar. There, you will see a heading that says "Make Money with Us" followed by a link that says, "Sell on Amazon." Click on that link and it will walk you through the systematic process of launching your Amazon Seller Central account.

Right away, you are going to be offered the decision to make an individual account or a professional account. You will notice that the individual account is free, while the professional account is $39.99 per month. Because you are just starting, it may seem tempting to launch a free account, but note that features such as Amazon FBA are not offered to individual account holders, as these accounts are geared more toward selling your own belongings in a "garage sale" type of business. If you want to run a real retail business through Amazon, you need to have a professional account, so you will need to pay the $39.99 fee to launch your account.

After you start your professional account, you will be required to provide information such as who you are, what login credentials you want to use, and what business you are associated with. You may also need to input important information linked to payment and taxes, which will allow Amazon to pay you your profits and offer you a tax slip come tax season. Make sure that you fill out all of this information now, in advance, so that it is ready to go when you begin paid or when it is time for you to declare your taxes at the end of the year.

After you have taken these actions, your Amazon Seller Central account will be created! You will not need to do anything further with your account until you are ready to begin ordering and listing products, at which point you will need the account to complete these parts of the process.

Chapter 6 Branding Your Product & Making It Stand Out

In this section I will be covering how you can create a 'brand' for your product which will develop brand loyalty in the long term.

Naming Your Product

Before you order your product, you will need to have a name for it - a brand that can be seen on Amazon, or any other channels/websites that you use. Here are some tips to come up with a great name for your product.

Don't get hung up: come up with a range of ideas, but it's important to not get too picky - just go with something that works!

Relevant to the niche: You should make sure that your brand name fits in with your niche and target audience/demographic.

Domain name: Ideally, you want to be able to purchase the exact domain name for your brand name, so this is something to check when picking a name. I recommend getting a '.com' domain.

Trademark search: Another important factor to consider is to make sure your product name is unique. Search for 'us trademark search' on Google and you will be able to check if your product name is infringing on other trademarked terms. On top of this, make sure that no other products on Amazon are using the same names or close variations.

Designing Your Logo

You will also need a logo to go along with your product brand. Here are some tips for creating an effective logo:

Clean and simple: Keep your logo simple and professional. This will also help when having your logo printed on your product. You want your logo to be easily seen and recognized. Think about how the logo will actually look on the product.

Quality: Make sure you create a high-resolution logo that will ensure that the logo is clean when it is finally printed. I recommend having a resolution of at least 1000 x 1000 pixels.

Packaging Design

You may decide that you want to have specific packaging designed for your product. For example, you could have a custom branded box/bag - this helps to set your product apart from competitors, and consumers love this!

How to get the design work done

The great thing is that you don't need any design skills - you just need ideas that someone else can bring to life. I get my logos designed on fiverr.com, but there are other sites where you can find great designers such as Up-Work and People Per Hour.

Creating a Brand for the Future

Creating a brand is much more than creating a nice logo and packaging. To create a solid Brand you need to build on this by creating a vision for customer experience, vision of your company etc. You need to be instilling your vision and brand to customers in order to create a long-term reputation for your company. Another factor to consider is whether the brand you create can be relevant to other products within the same category or a similar category. This way you will be able to cross-promote your products in the future to get free traffic.

Making Your Product Stand Out

On top of developing strong branding for your product, you will need to make your product stand out - and this is especially crucial in a competitive market. The way to do this is to make slight tweaks to your products in order to make it stand out from the competition.

The tweaks that you make to your product can be very simple, and the best way to figure out what tweaks to make is by looking at the reviews of other products.

Negative reviews: Look at the negative verified reviews of the biggest competitive products. Are there any trends? Is this something you could easily fix on the product?

Positive reviews: Can you combine all the positive features into your product? Work out what customers like in other products and try to improve on this in your product.

Once you have some ideas for improving the product, go ahead and reach out to your supplier to see if they can incorporate these into your products, and what the associated costs are.

Other ways to tweak your product

Bundled Packages: You also have the option to combine your product with another low cost product which will help your product add more value than your competitors. For example, offering low cost face scrubbers with a face cream product.

Bonus offers: Another way to make your product stand out of the crowd is to create a high quality bonus package with extra free complementary information that is relevant to your product. For example, with many of my products I offer a free bonus eBook package that teaches people how to get the most of the product.

Choosing Your Final Product & Supplier

Choosing a Final Product

It's now time to start narrowing down and choosing a final product to make an order for. This can be tricky, so here are the criteria to go by to select the final winning product.

Profit: If one product makes more pure profit, then it is likely better to go with that product, but remember to take into account the other criteria that we have previously covered.

Opportunity: Does one product have a higher chance for growth than the other? Think about whether a product has other products that are complementary that you could also sell with your brand in the future.

Start-up capital: Very important - you need to choose a product that you can comfortably afford to finance. If one product is much more aligned with your budget and meets the other criteria, then I strongly suggest going with that product.

Although it's crucial that your product meets all the criteria, I also encourage you to take your gut instinct into account! Sleep on your product ideas and give yourself a bit of time to mull over them.

Choosing a Final Supplier

By now you would have spoken with a number of suppliers, but you will of course need to narrow this down to one.

Profit: Again, this is a crucial factor and you should sort your final supplier prospects by the total profit margins.

Quality: Make sure you obtain product samples from the supplier. Cross examine samples from different products. Does one stand out significantly? Try not to bias this decision by how much they cost. You can even do a blind test on someone you trust who doesn't know the cost of the products.

Your Experience with Suppliers: Consider how suppliers have acted when reaching out to them. Did they respond quickly and accurately? Did they have a good command of English? This is very important and will be especially crucial when progressing onto the next stages with them.

Operational factors: Compare the minimum order quantity, supplier ability, and lead-time between suppliers. The most important is lead-time - anything over 15 days can cause major issues, and can lead to you run out of inventory on Amazon.

By taking *everything* into account in this section, along with everything previously covered in the book, you should be able to narrow down to one product and one supplier. You are now ready to place your first order, and one step closer to building your highly profitable FBA business.

Chapter 7 Creating Your Product Listing

A crucial part of building a successful FBA business is having high quality and high converting product listings that stand out from the competition. You need to start building your product listing page while you are waiting for your product to be manufactured and shipped. This way, as soon as your product arrives into the Amazon fulfillment center you will be ready to start selling with a listing page that crushes your competition.

Keyword Optimization

Understanding the keywords that your customers are using to find your keywords is the most important step in optimizing your product listing page. These keywords will need to be in the product's title, description, and marketing strategies to efficiently drive the most traffic to your product.

Choosing your keywords: In order to discover the keywords that people are using to search for your product, there are key places to look and utilize.

Amazon Search Field - If you type in a product into the Amazon search bar and do not hit the enter key, you should see a list of suggestions for phrases to type. These are your keyword ideas for your products.

Here is an example for the jump rope product - along with your search you see multiple phrases that are related. Go ahead and write these down in a spreadsheet, as these will be very effective keywords to target in your product listing.

Google Keyword Planner

This is a great tool that anyone can use to find loads of keyword ideas that are related to your product. Simply sign up for an AdWords account and you can use the tool for free. Enter your product into the search bar and you will be provided with hundreds of related keywords. Pick and choose the ones that are most relevant to your product and then add these to your spreadsheet of keywords.

Your Competition

Most of the keywords for your product will be placed in title, bullet points, and description of your competitor's product listing ad. Narrow down all the keywords that they are targeting, are there any particular phrases that might not be the exact wording of your product but relevant? Start off with analyzing the top product in your niche, and start adding these to your keyword spreadsheet.

Fiverr

There are plenty of search engine optimization (SEO) specialists available to hire on Fiverr. If you hire one for a gig, they will be very effective in providing a targeted list of keywords for your product. This will save you time and it is definitely worth the small investment.

So go ahead and put in some work to put together a list of highly relevant and targeted keywords. This will effectively pave the way for starting to construct your product listing page.

Product Title

I will now be showing you how to craft the perfect title that will incorporate your targeted keywords, and draw in your targeted audience. Your product title is one of the most important aspects of your product listing page, which is why it is extremely important to optimize it. The product title is also a key opportunity to make your product stand out from your competitor's titles.

Product title details - Amazon titles need to be less than 200 characters. It is also important to know that Amazon will randomly grab keywords from your title and then include these in the URL for your product.

Product title tips:

Include your biggest primary keyword at the very beginning of your product title. This is very important for showing maximum relevancy to Amazon, which will help your product rank better in the search results.

Try to include as many other keywords in your title that you discovered and included in your spreadsheet when doing keyword research.

You do not need to repeat keywords in your product title. For example, if you have "Jump Rope Set" as your primary keyword, you do not need to add the keyword "Jump Rope" into your product title. Amazon will be able to detect the keywords within longer keywords and rank your product for all of those keywords.

Write for your customers! Although your product title needs to include as many of your targeted keywords, the title still needs to read well and be enticing for people to click on.

Follow the template below to create a very effective title for your product that will get your product ranked and convert sales.

A Perfect Title Formula:

Main Keyword - Other Relevant Keyword - Benefits & Features - Sales Copy

Make sure you use punctuation to make sure the title flows and reads well. The sales copy that you include should be a call-to-action, special offer, or a guarantee. This sales copy will convince customers to continue on to reading your product listing page. An example of this could be "#1 Jump Rope with Free Shipping".

So overall, use this formula create a product title that balances having enough keywords along with being readable to your prospective customers. Make sure you don't rush this - take your time to come up with a targeted and effective title that will pave the way for your sales!

Bullet Points

There is a bullet point section just below the price on your Amazon product page. Here you can add up to 5 bullet points that will highlight the crucial information that you want your customer to see. I certainly recommend utilizing all 5 bullet points as this is another key opportunity to get customers interested to read the rest of your product description.

Bullet point tips:

• Do your best to make the bullet points stand out. This can be done by using stars, capital lettering etc.

• Include the benefits of your products, not just the features. What are the main benefits of your product that your competitors' product may not offer?

• Highlight any special offers or bonuses that you have.

• Customers will always look at this section as it is just near the price. Use this as an opportunity to really sell your product to them!

• Don't forget to include your keywords in the bullet points. This will further help you to rank for your desired keywords.

• The first and the last bullet points are where the customer will look most. Use these to highlight your main benefits and offers.

Chapter 8 What Are the Best Ways to Launch Your Products?

Reviews Are Extremely Important

One of the most influential factors when it comes to sales are the reviews. If optimizing and advertising play a decisive role in making the product more visible and boosting the rankings, reviews are responsible for increasing the conversion rate. Shoppers are constantly looking for information regarding a merchandise, after all. Having a well-structured product description is a big plus because the buyers can find important details related to the goods, such as specifications and a nicely written description. If you can write it as a story, that is a bigger bonus. What they also want to find is the opinion of other buyers regarding your product. The reviews are valid social statements connected to your merchandise; in many cases, the shoppers consider them the most trustworthy. A few things that you can see in a customer's feedback are:

- user experience
- shipping
- quality of the product

The specialist reviewers like to write them as a list of advantages and disadvantages. They usually cover the points mentioned above, primarily if the product is user-friendly and it meets the customer's expectation related to quality and design, along with the delivery process itself. As users pop on this platform with a clear intention to buy products, the reviews are most influential when taking the decision to buy a product, assuming that the description and specifications already meet the buyer requirements. The more feedback you get, the more likely your product will sell. The A9 algorithm sees the reviews as extremely important, and it indexes them accordingly. As soon as you get your first review, this will mean an impressive boost in rankings. If you conduct your business in a niche with less competition, around ten to 20 sales should guarantee a spot for your product in the first two pages. Some merchants realized the importance of the reviews and tried to obtain them "artificially" by paying individuals to write reviews of products. This practice is not accepted by Amazon because it creates a fake image of a merchandise in front of customers. They have extremely strict terms and conditions related to this practice, but you can still find some tools to get honest reviews. Customers come first in Amazon's view; that's why they are focusing on achieving their satisfaction and protecting them from products of poor quality. If shoppers always consult the reviews when buying a merchandise online, merchants should also do that to improve the quality of their products and services. By listening to your customers (and consumers of your competitors), you can adjust and customize your products and services according to the needs of your customers. Sales may win you some people once, but the customer service and the quality of your product will give you their absolute loyalty. If you consider Amazon Retail, most of their consumers only use this platform to buy a broad range of products. They do not need to look anywhere else because they are extremely satisfied with the services and products provided by Amazon. At a lower scale, this is what you need to aim for. Furthermore, respecting the "voice" of your customers expressed through the reviews can undoubtedly help you achieve this objective.

Find Something to Boost Your Initial Sales

Let's consider that you are completely new to Amazon and want to make good money by selling high-quality goods to different buyers. At this point, you have the listings prepared, your content is optimized with keywords used in a natural manner, and you have very artistic photos well-structured and informative product description. However, you are still missing that special something to trigger your first sales. You know that you will be charged anyway by Amazon for your inventory, regardless if you make sales or not. As you are on this platform to sell goods, you can't afford to lose time so you need sales to start kicking immediately. In order to achieve this objective, besides optimizing your content, you will need to consider using Amazon Advertising to generate your first sales, particularly the Sponsored Products ads campaign. This involves setting buying special spots, which are extremely visible on the first page of results. It's also called Amazon PPC because you will place your product in that special spot, and you will pay for each click being made on your product. Since users are most likely interested to buy, they don't fool around when clicking on such an advertisement. If they like what they see, they will definitely buy a product. You need to set up your daily budget as well, which will cover a limited amount of clicks. This tool is your best chance of getting your first sales, making your first money on Amazon, and starting your journey to the top of the rankings.

Amazon Coupons

It's really hard to refuse a product that comes with a discount, especially when you are already interested in it or it is similar to the items that you are into. An interesting sale strategy is to have the first products sold for a lesser price to attract more shoppers towards your product. Of course, you merely can't sell all your existent inventory at a reduced rate; that's why it's important to set a limited amount of items that you want to sell for a discount. This a good way to make potential customers aware of your brand's merchandise. Traffic on Amazon can also be generated by external sources, such as your social media or business website. You can post an ad on Facebook or send customized emails to your customers from the database that you already have to announce your presence on Amazon and give them special offers. You can sweeten the deal by throwing in an Amazon coupon that's designated to provide a discount on one of your listed products on the platform. If you are hoping to get your first sales using this process, and let's say you have a few Amazon Coupons to give away, then you need to work intensively on this marketing campaign. After all, your presentation will need to reach more and more potential customers to become very effective. It's only up to you to choose your default sales trigger - whether you want to advertise through social media, send plenty of emails to your existing customers, give away discount coupons or choose the Amazon PPC option. Advertising on the platform can reach a higher number of customers compared to using external sources and offering coupons.

Follow Up to Get a Feedback

The most effective sale is the one that generates feedback because it creates all the necessary conditions to climb up on rankings, increase product visibility, and eventually generate other sales. In the old days of trade, sales were done through recommendations as well. The "word of mouth" was spread, and more and more people were aware of a specific product and its advantages. Sales triggered other sales, in other words. Things are about the same when it comes to online selling platforms, considering reviews and feedback are proven methods to produce more sales. The ideal situation is to get either after every sale, but it is genuinely hard to think of a seller which has achieved this performance. Reviews and feedback boost the popularity of the product and brand awareness, and shoppers are most likely to buy famed items because they are already considered trustworthy. A piece of good advice is to follow up with the customer to find out what he or she thinks about the merchandise. In the eyes of the shoppers, after all, it proves that you care about them and that you are willing to go the extra mile to satisfy their needs. This is the way to get positive feedback and reviews, which is something that Amazon and the users that are present on this platform appreciate very much. Another good idea is to comment on a customer review directly, thanking them for their opinion.

Chapter 9 Packing and Setting Up Shipments To Amazon

Now that you've listed your items and had them setup for sale through Fulfillment by Amazon, it's time to prepare your boxes to ship. Do not skimp or skip anything during this process, as your success depends on your ability to follow Amazon's requirements to ensure everything goes smoothly.

Step 1. Clean Everything

If you're selling any used goods or new goods with dust on the boxes, you'll unfortunately have to take the time to clean them up prior to packaging and shipping them. This part can seem like a time waster, but sending dirty products to customers is an easy way to get poor reviews and lose future business.

Start by removing any price tags. You do not want them to know that you paid a fraction of the cost they paid. To remove any of the sticky residue, you can use products like Goo Gone or just a little rubbing alcohol if it won't damage the packaging. Be careful while removing labels and cleaning, as any imperfects will make the item appear used even if it isn't.

Step 2. Prepping Your Items

If the item is in retail packaging that's undamaged, you can easily leave it as is. If it isn't, you will need to box or bag your product before placing any barcode labels on them. It is recommended that you bubble wrap items before bagging them. Boxing items when it's unnecessary should be avoided, as the costs are much too high for little in return.

Step 3. Labeling Items

Labeling is the next important step. Per the earlier recommendation, Avery 5160 (30) size labels are perfect for this application.

To print your labels, return to your product inventory by logging in at Seller Central, and clicking "Products Amazon Fulfills" under the "Inventory" tab. This will bring you to a page with all of your products awaiting labels and shipping. From here, check the items you are going to ship, and then from the drop down menu above or below, choose "Print Item Labels."

The following page will show you the items, and at the bottom is a drop down menu that lets you choose the printing method and label sizes. If you've chosen to use the Avery 5160 (30) sized labels, it should automatically be chosen as the default. Once you're prepared, click "Print Item Labels."

Here, Amazon will remind you that you'll be placing these barcode labels over the existing barcodes. If the barcode area is too small for your label, you can cover it with a white label and place the barcode elsewhere, but you MUST cover the existing barcode.

The result is a PDF that's downloadable, which you can then print. The barcodes should be easy to manage since they include the name of the item on them in most situations. If the item is cleaned and ready, place this barcode over the original barcode, follow the notes you took earlier concerning Amazon's requirements for packaging (remember, some items must be bagged or boxed per their requirements), and place it in the correct box for shipping. Repeat this with all of your products until you're ready to ship.

Note that you can setup labeling by Amazon instead. This costs $0.20 per label, so it's a huge waste of your money since labeling really doesn't take very long at all. Only do this if you're selling massive quantities and really don't have the time or can't hire someone to help out.

Step 4. Shipping Your Box

Now that you've labeled all your items, fulfilled Amazon's requirements for packaging, and placed the items in the box securely, it's time to finally ship to Amazon for their fulfillment services. You've made it. This is almost time to celebrate a little!

Returning to your FBA inventory, you should be able to select all the items you've already labeled, and then from the drop down menu, choose "Send/Replenish Inventory."

Since we've already labeled and prepped our items, we can click "Review Shipments" on the follow page. This should tell you the places each item needs to go along with the name of the shipment. Note that you won't always be sending all products to the same distribution warehouse, so it's important not to package up your boxes before this step.

If you have more than a single shipment package on this page, you can click the "View contents" link beside each of the shipments to be made to see which products should go in which box. Package up your boxes as you go. Do not seal your boxes yet.

If everything is in the box where it belongs, choose "Approve Shipments," and you'll be able to purchase shipping for your packages. To finish this step, you'll have to weigh and measure your boxes, input this data into the shipping page, and select the appropriate carrier for the job. Most of the time, UPS is the route to go. Click "calculate" and Amazon will give you pricing and the option to print out your shipping labels.

You can simply tape your labels onto your boxes, but if you prefer adhesive printer paper, the best size for these box labels is Avery 8465, which has an adhesive label on each side of a standard sized sheet of printer paper. Once printed, remove both of the labels and place them on the box in a way that they cannot be sliced down the middle while it's being opened by Amazon's warehouse staff. Generally, the two top halves of the box are perfect. Take it to the UPS drop off, do a little celebratory dance, and start working on finding new products to continue growing your business. Amazon will let you know once your products have arrived and are ready for sale!

Chapter 10 Amazon FBA and Tax Season

Amazon FBA is a business that will require you to file taxes. You might be wondering how you can file taxes with Amazon FBA, including what tax forms you will need and what you need to track in order to submit your taxes clearly and precisely. In this chapter, we are going to summarize what needs to be done come tax season for you to properly file your Amazon FBA business so that you are compliant with what is required of you as a business owner.

When it comes to filing taxes for your Amazon FBA business, it is truly not that challenging. If you have ever filed as a self-employed individual before, you will be pleased to find that it is not much different than filing for your own business. If you are new to filing for yourself, you might want to book with a tax agent who can help you file your taxes properly so that you do not make any mistakes in your filing process.

Using the Amazon 1099-K Tax Form

1099-K tax forms are forms that help the IRS know how much money you have made monthly, as well as annually, through your business. Individuals who are filing on their own will often file 1099-K forms to track their income through their own businesses. Fortunately for you, Amazon also uses the 1099-K to track information relating to sales, taxes, and shipping fees. This means that if you are a professional seller who is selling large quantities of products through Amazon, your form will already be filled out through Amazon's employees as they manage your products. All you have to do, then, is print off the 1099-K and use it to file your taxes.

If you are an individual seller, or if you do not make a significant amount through your business in any given year, chances are you will not receive a 1099-K because you did not make enough money through your business to file it. For the 1099-K, there is a threshold of $20,000 that needs to be met in order for Amazon to fill it out. If you do not meet that threshold, Amazon will not fill it out for you, and you will not receive one.

It is important to realize that if you have more than $20,000 in sales, Amazon will be filing a 1099-K form for your business, which means the IRS already knows that you have a business with Amazon. If you fail to report this income or if you report it incorrectly, you could be audited due to your discrepancy. Pay attention and make sure that your numbers match the ones on the 1099-K generated by Amazon so that you do not find yourself being audited.

As well, even if you do not receive a 1099-K, you still must file taxes on all of the income that you received from Amazon. It will still count toward your overall annual income, and it just won't qualify you for a 1099-K to be filled out and provided to you from Amazon.

What Qualifies as Income

The IRS is going to track your gross annual income through Amazon, which is going to include everything that you earned, including your revenue, not just your profits. Any numbers relating to your income, including shipping charges and anything else you receive, are all going to be listed on your 1099-K, even if you did not receive all of these funds directly into your bank account.

If you are not sure about the numbers, or if you have never filed this way before, filing with a consultant can help you keep track of your numbers more effectively so that you do not make any mistakes and pay for it later on. Always trust the numbers that come in on your 1099-K because, at the end of the day, Amazon was responsible for helping you with all of the income, which means that their state-of-the-art systems are likely more accurate than your own.

Reporting Income Outside the US

If you are selling on Amazon outside of the US, you are not liable for US taxes, which means that you are not going to receive a 1099-K form from Amazon. What you will need to do is provide a W-8BEN form to Amazon which is going to exempt Amazon from having to report your income for tax purposes.

For anyone selling outside of the US, you are going to have to track your own income and file according to your country's unique tax laws. Again, it is still important that you report and pay taxes on your Amazon income as not doing so could result in serious penalties for lying on your taxes.

Tracking Amazon Tax Deductions

Anyone who runs their own business qualifies for certain tax deductions throughout the year. Typically, any expense that contributes to you running your own business is going to be considered a tax deduction, so it is important that you keep all of your receipts relating to your business. Keep receipts from everyone, such as your suppliers, your shipping companies, Amazon, and any promotional or marketing expenses that you pay. Anything that directly contributes to you making an income on Amazon can be considered a tax deduction, so feel free to note this down in your taxes.

It is important that you keep the receipts for any tax deduction that you make on your business. Receipts provide evidence that these funds were spent and that you did put the money toward running your business. If you do not have them, even if the money was spent on your business, you might run into problems later on should the IRS decide to audit you. Avoid these problems by keeping your business receipts for seven years so that any audits made are able to be proven and reported through your saved receipts.

Chapter 11 Tools That You Will Need to Get Started

You already know what Amazon FBA is. Let us have a quick brief of the process again. If you are a seller, you need to list your products for sale on the website of Amazon with a well calculated price that benefits you as well as the Amazon. Then, you have to ship your merchandize to the warehouse of Amazon. When a customer makes a purchase of your products, they get the shipping from Amazon and the company also handles the communication with the customers. And Amazon profits by charging a cut from the sale and a small amount of fees. The process will keep on running unless you want to stop it.

To get into flow with this business with Amazon, you must have some essential things handy. These supplies and tools will make your business easier and you will also earn more with time. However, it is not necessary that you must procure these tools in the beginning of your business. Moreover, many of these tools are tax deductible. Thus, you can take the help of these tools for last minute tax deductions. That is good news! Isn't it?

1.   Inventory lab

Inventory lab is a web application which runs separately from your internet browser. Though it can work with any operating system and computer, it is recommended that you use it with at least Internet Explorer 8 and a modern browser. The application will support your work in terms of innovation and customer service. Inventory lab is capable of handling monthly profit/ loss, goods sold, etc. The additional Scanning Application of Inventory Lab is also listed in the list of essential tools at #2!

2.   Scoutify

This application deals with scanning of items you list on Amazon. You will find Scoutify as a part of the previous application, Inventory Lab. The user interface of Scoutify is very simple to navigate. You will also find many features that will make your scanning portion of the business simpler than ever before. One exciting feature of the app is that if you receive multiple results after scanning an item, you do not have to scan the product again. You can simply go back to the results to verify the duplication of results.

3.   Gummed Tape Dispenser

An efficient tape dispenser is indispensable when you are working with someone as big as Amazon. Your customers will be pleased when they see the product packed in a professional manner. The recommended product to buy is Better Pack 333. The product is a gummed tape dispenser. Recall the kind of tapes on the packages of Amazon. This tape dispenser gives you the same kind of tapes. You will need only one portion of tape on both opening of your box. The dial on the tape dispenser gives you the perfect tape each time you enter the size of the tape required.

4.   Scan-Fob 2006

It is a 1D barcode scanner that you can hold in your hand and use it conveniently. It can be used to send data to various devices like iPhone and Android devices. This wireless Bluetooth laser barcode scanner lets you scan the barcode from a much longer distance than you expect. Thus, you do not have to take down every item from the top shelf of your garage to scan the barcode. It sounds superfluous but it really makes your business easier.

5.   E-bates

E-bates is a Cashback website and helps you a lot in online arbitrage. You can install it in your browser bar which will constantly remind you to activate cash back if you are working on a retail website. E-bates is more reliable in terms of giving you Cashbacks in time, which many other Cashback websites do not do.

6.   Self-Sealing Poly Bags

If you are dealing in smaller items like health and beauty items and groceries, you will definitely need a lot of self-sealing poly bags. You must keep bags in 4 sizes handy- 8_10, 9_12, 11_14 & 14_20. You can get 100 of each size of these bags from Amazon itself.

7.   Price Blink

If you want help with online sourcing, this tool is indispensable. You can add it in your browser bar and it will let you know about a product that you are searching for, if it is available for lower prices on other websites. Thus, you can also search websites that are not very popular for options of buying. It also notifies you of the coupon codes for the websites which you are currently using. Price Blink comes absolutely free!

8.   Dymo Label Writer

Dymo label writer is a very efficient solution for professional labeling, mailing and filing needs. You will save a lot of time with this tool at your disposal. You just need to connect this label writer to your computer and you can print labels directly from Outlook or Microsoft Word and many other famous programs. The thermal printing technology of the product eliminates the expense of toner or ink. You can also print expiration dates on grocery items and do many more things with it. Look for this product in a yard sale to save money.

9.   Laser printer

A printer is an equally indispensable tool like a scanner. And, if it is a laser printer, nothing like it! It prints your papers quickly and saves you a lot of money since you do not have to buy ink frequently. You can even buy a wireless printer if your pocket allows. There are a lot of things to be printed in a business and a printer makes your business simpler.

10. Scotty peelers

They come in handy, really handy if you deal with liquidation products, or cut down boxes, or open cartons of online sourcing; which is quite obvious that you will do in Amazon FBA. You can even buy multiple Scotty Peelers and you will never have enough of them. The metal peelers are better than the plastic ones.

11. Amazon seller app

You can use this app to find out the probability of profits when you are making a purchase. It gives you comprehensive information about the number of sellers for the item that you are planning to list, the sales rank or if Amazon itself is selling the product. Thus, it helps you take a better decision in all aspects.

There are of course many more tools than those on the list. But, these are the essential things that you must have if you are going to start your Amazon FBA.

Chapter 12 Make Your First $1,000 On FBA

Following my story with getting my toes wet in FBA and making a huge amount of mistakes, it seems wise to give you a plan of action to make your first $1,000-2,000 on FBA. Hindsight is always 20/20, and this is how I wish I had started things off because it would have taught me all the lessons I learned the hard way.

Step 1. Gather Supplies, Sign Up, Upgrade to Professional Plan

We've went over all the items you'll need to get started, so begin there, and while you're waiting for items to ship or once you're ready to move forward, sign up for your seller account and download the Amazon Seller app. Upgrade to the professional plan on Seller Central. It will cost you $40, but for this plan to work, we really want to sell more than 40 items anyway.

Step 2. Clean Out Your Closets

For your first $1,000, at least part of this should simply be items around your house that you don't really need. This includes DVDs, CDs, records, video games, books, electronics, anything you got for Christmas but never used, etc. This should make up at least a roughly estimated $250 of your first $1,000. Use the Amazon Seller app to scan these items, and use the revenue calculator to estimate your earnings. If you can't make it to roughly $250, you'll need to overcompensate a bit on the next steps.

Go ahead and list these items for sale. If there are enough to bother with a shipment, ship them for fulfillment, and the earning will begin while you continue.

Step 3. Hit the Ground Running with Retail Arbitrage

While I think most successful FBA sellers eventually move away from going into every store and scanning anything that seems to be on sale, this really is the best way to start out. The risk/reward is lower than trying to jump headfirst into wholesale.

Where I live, this would mean going to the SPCA thrift shop, Goodwill, Walmart, Target, Lowes, Home Depot, Big Lots, Ross, TJ Maxx, Kohls, and many others. If there is a shopping center around, starting here is great since so many stores are located together and don't require a ton of gas or time simply traveling around. Outlet malls are even better.

Do not buy anything that cannot be sold at a price of three times the amount you've paid for it. You won't always have time to calculate actual profits while you're shopping, so this rule of thumb is your best bet to avoid losing any money on products that aren't worth selling.

This process could take a few days, but you should be able to calculate another opportunity for earnings of at least $250, if not significantly more.

Step 4. Facebook, Craigslist, Free Stuff

You should be shopping Craigslist pretty religiously. Not only can you sometimes find great deals, but you can also post ads for certain items that you believe will sell. Additionally, there are a lot of free listings on Craigslists, and while many of the items may not be worth a ton of money, they are free, so if they're viable to sell, the cost of shipping isn't really a huge concern. Try to take advantage of these while remembering that light items are better to sell than heavy items.

Unless you live in the middle of nowhere (and sometimes even if you do), you likely have a handful of Facebook groups that service people buying, selling, and trading in your area. Take advantage of these as well. Much like Craigslist, you can post ads for the types of things you'd like to buy and resell.

This method should easily be able to bring in an additional $250 worth of profit in products.

Step 5. Yard Sales and Flea Market

On the weekend, get up early and make your way to any yard sales and flea markets you can. The generally low prices at these sales are going to make for a lot of easy profit if you find anything decent. If you find a box or pile of items you might be able to sell, try to buy the entire thing for a deeply discounted rate.

For example, if someone has a nice selection of roughly 50 DVDs priced for $1 a piece, offer them $25 to take them all off their hands at once. This particular example works well at yard sales. The worst they can do is tell you, "No thanks," and if you're lucky they'll meet you somewhere in the middle.

If there are any multi-family yard sales or church rummage sales, you absolutely should be attending them. These tend to have lower prices and great amount of variety.

Again, you should fairly easily be able to net the remaining $250 worth of profit from products through this method. In fact, if you've done all four of these methods for sourcing products over a two-week period, I'd be surprised if you didn't end up with more than $1,000 worth of profits should everything sell.

Step 6. List and Ship to Amazon, Wait for Profits.

Anything that hasn't been listed and shipped to Amazon, go ahead and do that now. If you haven't reached an estimated worth of $1,000, just repeat the steps above throughout the next week, and you should be able to make up the difference.

Step 7. Take Notes

This is really the importance of the "your first $1,000" exercise. Your first $1,000 is just a small milestone in a long list of success stories you will have. What you learn from non-discriminately shopping pretty much every local resource available is that what seems to work for you may not be what works for others. Which of the items that caught your eye were actually extremely viable? Which ones sold immediately after the listing went live, and which sat around (or remain in storage still)? All of this is important because for your next $1,000, you will now know what to ask for when you post ads on Craigslist to buy stuff. You will also know what to stop and look at when you're browsing through a yard sale, which stores seem to produce well for you, and you're beginning to learn how to interact with people through social media in a laid back but semi-professional manner. Ultimately, you may have worked pretty hard for that first $1,000, especially in regards to time, but the information you learned along the way is the real payout.

Chapter 13 Delays

In regards to possible delays, it is fair to mention that you should be aware right from the beginning, even at the stage of supplier research.

You might be having a Friday afternoon, and feel like contacting your first suppliers to see how they respond, and you might not get any reply for a week from any of them. Instead of giving up the whole supplier research or thinking about what did you do wrong, you might be better-off looking up the Chinese calendar first.

In China holidays might differ according to where you live, and you should not only be aware, but also understand what they mean, and respect that.

I personally even write them messages like; have a good rest while on holiday and to all Factory workers too, but it's not necessarily at all.

Some of these holidays are not really chosen, but due to the Government, it's been forced on everyone to shut down all the factories.

Holidays can cause issues at both end of the Businesses, the factory and you as an Amazon FBA seller. When you place an ordor, make sure you don't run out of stock.

As you see sometimes, production might delay for a week or two. If you are not prepared properly, once you have no inventory at

Amazon, you will lose your ranking, as well as loose profit, and many customers who might go buy a similar product. And next time they may buy the same other brand rather than look for you to know if you are back in stock.

Chinese holidays are important to take note of. There are also times that huge events take place in China that you should also be aware of, as some of them can even kill your business like many Amazon FBA sellers experienced when the Olympics took place in China in 2008.

The pollution is very high in China, so anytime a big event takes place, the Government takes extra measures by closing most factories in order to have a better looking sky.

It doesn't really matter where you source from, however you should watch the news and understand external causes of possible delays.

In regards to AIR shipping there are few days of delays that I have experienced, literally 1 or 2 days. It happened with DHL, as the Duty had to be paid before delivery, and I had to reschedule the delivery. I wasn't able to reschedule for Saturday, so I had to wait from Friday till Monday, knowing that my product was sitting at DHL's ware house since the Friday afternoon instead of me actually doing my quality checks.

Sea shipping will always take at least 4-6 weeks, if you source from China to the US, and possible delays might take another week or two.

Also, when sourcing by Sea Shipping, same as Air Shipping, Duties must be paid before picking up your shipment, or sending a freight forwarder for collection, and that is the most convenient option.

Also when importing with Sea Shipping, there are some busy times where public holidays could cause port congestion and your shipment could be delayed.

Always communicate with your suppliers to avoid any possible delays, as you might not have experienced. However, your supplier might be able to suggest good times for shipping, since they may know more about local news and Shipping Agencies than you.

Clearance paperwork can also cause delay before your product is released. So it's a good idea to be ready with all the documents that is required for this purpose on time, and make sure there are no errors on any of the documentations that you will provide as all that might just cause you additional delays.

In a perfect situation, to be able to source from any country to another should take no time, however there are so many steps, and so many companies are involved that for most of them you or your supplier are not special at all, and if they find something incorrect or against their procedure, it will cause a great loss of money to your Business.

Chapter 14 e-bay Vs. Amazon

Usually, there is no competition between the two platforms. The real thing is dependent on you and what you really want. This might sound somehow strange, so let's take a knife to it and break it down.

eBay

Over the years, eBay is like one mighty flea market, the sellers are doing most if not all of the jobs, like setting up your 'stand.' You will handle transactions, offer product, ship it, and perform all the things involved to make sales and purchase a complete chain. You have a 100% responsibility here.

The reason why this chapter begins with 'it's up to you' is that though it seems like a lot of work, there are benefits in it. One of the advantages is that you will earn more when you are doing more of the work. A larger percentage of the profit will be completely yours, or you will be having more of it than in a situation where someone else or a team is handling it for you.

Amazon FBA

We aren't looking at Amazon as a whole but Amazon FBA specifically. So how does that look like in the setting we are talking about?

This is like one big mall where you own a shop. There are storekeepers who work for everyone and help them sell their items. Once you sign up for the program, you will get a space in the warehouse. You will pay for it of course, but it also means that when you are at home sleeping or watching your favorite show, some is handling shipping, packing and delivering your items to your buyer's location.

Of course, the benefit is more than that, and we have explained most of it. The most important one we should talk about here are the charges you will pay for using the services.

Well, you can sell on both channels using Amazon.

You haven't forgotten Multi-Channel Fulfillment, have you? You will keep your item with Amazon, and they will do the job of shipping and delivering the item when people make an order on Amazon or on the other platforms.

Go to your seller account. Choose to create Multi-Channel Shipment to a channel like eBay. Let Amazon fill the submitted orders. They will also manage the orders you have submitted. Things will even be easier if you are using a professional account. Amazon can automatically fulfill the FBA inventory with MCF.

Chapter 15 How to Use Seller Central To Upload Inventory, Create Shipping Plan, Get Paid, and...

Using Amazon Seller Central is not that complicated as it seems to be. Let us see how you can use it.

Using Seller Central to get Payments

For initiating transmission of funds to your bank account from your seller account, Amazon Payments needs:

- Valid information of your credit card for billing and verification purposes.
- Valid information concerning your bank account to which you want the funds to be transferred.

After a sale takes place, and you confirm with Amazon that you have shipped the order, Amazon starts the process of payment from the account of buyer. However, in the case that it is an Amazon FBA order, Amazon will credit your account once they shipped out the order. The net proceeds of the sale are credited to your account. It is also important to note that the refunds to customers and selling fees are debited against the funds credited to your account.

The payments in your seller account are credited every 14 days. Amazon transfers the funds once Amazon Payments deduces that your funds do not need to be held to cover the charges, A-to-Z guarantee claims, refunds or other declarations against your transactions of sales. For receiving payments, you must mention the details of a US checking account/ UK bank account/ Eurozone bank account (Austria, Cyprus, Estonia, Belgium, Finland, France, Greece, Ireland, Germany, Italy, Luxembourg, the Netherlands, Malta, Portugal, Slovenia, Slovakia, and Spain)/ New Zealand, Australia, India, Canada or Hong Kong.

When you need to ship your orders yourself

Amazon handles all the packaging, labelling and shipping on its own for your Amazon FBA products. But if you are working under the process of Amazon Merchant Shipping, you have to handle the shipping yourself.

Shipping, managing and selling your products

You can put buttons and allow clicks on your websites to sell your merchandize. You can check your requests and orders daily with the help of "Manage Orders" in Seller Central. You must ship the orders as soon as possible to gain customer loyalty.

Confirm the shipments

You need to confirm your shipment with Amazon and tell them the details of date of sending, the carrier used and other tracking information regarding the package. If you confirm the shipment, Amazon charges the customers. And, if you do not verify the shipment, your payment will not be initiated. The order is cancelled if you do not initiate the shipment after 30 days of order. You must sign in to Seller Central often. A notice will be displayed on the home page if any of your orders are in danger of cancellation.

Inventory Loader

If you want to upload multiple listings in one file to match against existing pages of products, you have to use Inventory Loader at Amazon.com. You cannot use it to create new pages of products. You can add new stock, amend existing items, and delete or "zero" your stock for items that are not available. You can also cleanse and replace all your listings with one upload only.

Since you are only modifying your stock, you do not have to provide product data in complete detail as you would when you use a category specific file of inventory. You can also use Inventory Loader to upload and modify your listings in multiple categories of products at the same time.

Using Seller Central to create Shipping Creation Workflow

You can create your shipment to the fulfillment centers of Amazon with the following steps of shipping creation workflow:

- Place Quantity
- Put Products In order
- Label Products
- Preview Consignment
- Prepare Consignment
- Summary

First of all, you need to choose your products in the inventory you want to ship to the company. You can do it using the "Manage FBA Inventory" or "Manage Inventory" page of the Seller Central. Select the product you want to transport, choose Send/ Replenish Inventory from the drop down menu of "Apply to Selected Items(s)" on Manage FBA Inventory page. The next page of Send/ Replenish Inventory will require you to take the following decisions:

Make a shipping plan/ Add to an Open Shipping Plan: In case you have an existing shipping plan, you can choose the plan from the drop down plan after you select "Add to an Existing Shipping Plan".

Verify your ship-from address: The address you had entered can be used to ship your consignment. If you wish to edit it, you can enter a fresh ship-from address.

Select the type of packing: You need to select case-packed products or individual products.

After you are done with all these steps, select "Continue to shipping plan" tab to start your workflow.

Send your FBA Inventory to Amazon

After you are set to send your inventory to Amazon, the next step is to create a shipping plan. It is a list of items which you wish to send to the fulfillment centers of Amazon. Your seller account has a shipment creation tool, which makes it simpler to select the items you wish to send, your shipment method, the quantity of the products, whether you wish to label the products yourself or Amazon should do it. You can also procure printable shipping and product labels from the shipping creation tools along with the guidance to prepare your items for shipment.

Once you are ready with your shipment plan, you can start preparing and packing your items in order to ship them to the Amazon fulfillment centers. You can break your shipping plan into various multiple shipments, which are directed to different Amazon fulfillment centers. This brings your products closer to your customers in different regions.

Chapter 16 How to Create Bundle To Eliminate Competition

You cannot ignore the competition on Amazon even if you want to. There are many fast selling products on Amazon which can overtake your products if you become lazy and do not take the competition seriously. People often become tired of competing with the swarm of sellers on your product page of Amazon. You need to look for different ways to raise your margins and trade more products. If you aspire that you had something exclusive to offer on the website, you need to take one step ahead. You do not need to private label or import your products to stand ahead of the crowd. You just need to create your own Amazon bundles. You must be wondering what are Amazon bundles.

Amazon bundles are exclusive products which you build yourself by joining two or more compatible, existing products into one bundle. Retail arbitrage products can be bundled together. Wholesale products can be bundled together. Imported products can also be bundled. Moreover, you can also bundle together all the three kinds of products.

Bundling the products together is a very effective method to stay ahead, at least three steps, of the competition. You do not need to have a very high budget for creating bundles.

Use your present method of sourcing to create bundles

You can sell your bundle and earn higher margin since you have an exclusive product in demand. Sometimes, several units are sold in just one day. You can own the product page of Amazon and the Buy Box as well. This keeps you ahead of competition. You can also create high demand by creating bundles of seasonal products. Moreover, you do not have to look for new providers of products if you repurpose saturated inventory. All your products can be sold in all categories of Amazon even if you offer entry level bundles or premium bundles.

The hurdles with bundles

Creating bundles does sound great but it is not so simple. Every bundle is not created equally. Not any random products can be bundled and sold like that. They will not sell for sure. You need to know what products you should bundle together to make maximum profits.

Important things to note while creating bundles

You must create bundles of products which are in demand. Create the product page of Amazon correctly so that buyers can easily find it in their search. It is equally important to price the bundles correctly to hit on target. Overpriced bundles will not sell. Choose the correct goods to bundle together. If you do not know how to bundle goods, you must go through the guidelines of bundling by Amazon. Otherwise, your listings may be cancelled. Another most important thing is to pass your bundle through the test of profitability factor.

A perfect bundle is the one which gives maximum value to the customers and the products are complimentary to each other. You must read the *Amazon's Product Bundling Policy in Seller Central* before you proceed to create your own bundles. You will also need to buy your own UPC (Universal Product Code) to list your bundle on Amazon.

When a bundle cannot be called a bundle?

A multi-pack cannot be categorized as a bundle. For example, you cannot call eight pairs of white socks as a bundle. If a bundle is just a variation of the parent product, you cannot call it a bundle.

When you do not need to buy a UPC

If your products fall into the following categories, you do not require buying a new UPC. The UPC on the product itself can be used.

☐ Home & Garden

Kitchen & Dining

Bedding & Bath

Furniture & Décor

Appliances

Arts, Sewing & Crafts

Lawn, Patio & Garden

Home Improvement

Pet Supplies

Lamps & Light Fixtures

Hand & Power Tools

Bath & Kitchen Fixtures

Building Supplies

Hardware

Grocery & Gourmet Foods

Sports & Outdoors

Outdoor Recreation

Fitness & Exercise

Cycling

Fishing & Hunting

Boating & Water Sports

Outdoor & Athletic Clothing

Team Sports

Sports Collectibles

Fan Shop

Golf

All Outdoors & Sports

If your products fall beyond these categories mentioned above, you would require buying a new UPC in favor of your multipack.

Chapter 17 Understanding Amazon's Success

Chances are you're fairly familiar with Amazon from the perspective of a buyer. They sell goods from a multitude of companies, including individuals who list their own items, and offer everything from digital products like music and e-books to physical products like home goods, toys, video games, and almost anything you can possibly think of ordering.

As the name might suggest, Amazon is huge much like the body of water that it's named after. Every single month they average more than 65 million buyers. That's 65 million customers all spending money through one interface, on one website, every single month. A large part of their success has been marketing and fulfilling those marketing promises, such as secure shopping, comparably low prices, and perks like free shipping for orders that qualify. In addition, Amazon has such a large array of items that it can almost virtually replace the need to ever leave the home to shop.

The largest reason Amazon is successful is because they are customer-centric. They cater to the buyer. As businessmen have always said, "The customer is always right." Amazon has lived by this motto while still going out of their way to improve the seller's experience as well.

Why You Should Use Amazon as a Seller

While being a buyer-oriented online shopping experience means that the buyer is almost always going to be able to get the upper-hand in disputes and other exchanges, it is still of the utmost importance to realize that Amazon is often the best possible place to sell your goods online. This is true for a couple reasons.

Firstly, Amazon has locked down the concept of the all-encompassing online shopping portal, and taking advantage of its many ways to produce an income is well documented and relatively easy compared to creating an online store or other online service from scratch. Their one-stop shopping experience provides more than you can provide on your own website, and unless you're ready to invest millions of dollars and years of hard work, it's unlikely that you'll be able to effectively compete with them on your own.

Secondly, the costs of getting started are minimal when compared to setting up your own online sales channels. While it may be tempting to try to avoid Amazon's fees, the truth is that a higher sales volume on Amazon and the initial cost of startup and maintaining a seller presence is much more expensive than these fees will typically be. Even if you are going to start an online store yourself, not having an Amazon presence means lost opportunities to reach the largest number of buyers in the world. Since the costs are lower to start with Amazon, it's obviously the best choice to start here and work on expanding later if that is your goal.

New and Used

One great advantage of Amazon, for both buyers and sellers, is that they not only list items that are brand new, but they also list items that are in various conditions. Having the option to sell used (and sometimes even rare) items through a safe and secure platform like Amazon means that nearly anything can be sold or bought through the same platform. While the ability to price the items you sell (and see everyone else's pricing) means more competition, this isn't as huge of a concern as one might think. We'll talk about that more later.

Customer Involvement

Another great thing about Amazon is that with a large amount of customers comes a huge amount of people that are interacting with the website past the point of purchase. This extends past simply writing reviews, but these reviews are of the utmost importance.

Traditionally, a person would go into a store, look at a product, possibly get to handle it for a few moments, and then have to decide if the price tag fit their expectations and limited knowledge of the item. This not only takes a lot of time, but the results are lackluster at best. There are very few ways to decide if a $1,000 laptop is worth $500 more than the $500 laptop sitting directly next to it. This is especially true if their technical specs are relatively similar. The internet has improved this through the use of customer reviewers. When it comes to customer reviews,

Amazon tends to have the most reviews available per product when compared to other sites. This is true because they have a huge customer base, but it is also true because Amazon actively encourages members to take the time to let others know if they were happy with a product or not.

This translates into more sales for products that review well with purchasers. Where a dedicated website for selling products may be able to provide a really well written review from the content creators, the huge amount of customers willing to post reviews on Amazon can sometimes lead to HUNDREDS of opinions on a product. Similarly, when a product is bought a lot, it is hoisted to the top of the best seller lists that Amazon generates based on automated algorithms. As a seller, this means that if you are looking to pick up products that are highly desirable, it is easy for you to determine what products (or at least what type of products) are being sold regularly. This customer involvement and automated calculations done by Amazon allows you some detailed insight into the market(s) you are most likely to venture into.

Next, let's discuss the difference between selling on Amazon and selling on Amazon using their Fulfillment by Amazon services.

Chapter 18 Quality Control

Quality control is something that you should always have in mind.

Confirming the product at your first order is only one little part when talking about quality control. In fact, you should be thinking about quality control already when searching for suppliers.

I already mentioned earlier that once you are searching for suppliers on Alibaba, you should always find out where do they supply the most and you can always ask. However, even before reaching out to them on Alibaba there is a click of a button that will give you a nice overview of the factory's main transaction history.

With this example I can already assume that it might not be a good idea to use this supplier if you want to sell the product in Japan or Germany.

Of course you might take the advantage of being the first who does it. However, the standards and people's requirements differ in many countries.

I am relating this example to quality control already as some products are considered to be a good quality in the US, but might be very low for the UK, or vice versa.

As for a supplier who provides low prices, and thinking that will make it on the US market, you should make sure that the main transaction history for the same supplier is indeed the US market.

Next, you should be ordering samples as I explained before by comparing multiple suppliers' product as well as making sure they are using safe packaging for delivery.

Once you have chosen the right supplier and already private labeled your sample product, you must be very vigilant and try to find as many mistakes as possible, faults, or defects right at the beginning.

In case there is a problem or fault with the OEM sample order and you assume that in higher volume those defects will disappear, then you really should think again.

Any careless attitude you display will reflect on your product, and your suppliers will never spend more money on your product, neither will they work harder unless you make them do so.

That being said, you must always exhibit an attitude towards your product like a real business, and always look at the quality, and if there is any direction you want to go it is only to create better and better quality, and your suppliers must be on the same page.

In order to make sure that your suppliers are always on the same page with you, everything must be documented, not only to remind them about your expectations, but to make sure they understand who dictates the terms in regards to the quality.

I do understand that there are some awesome employees out there who never required being baby sited; how-ever you can only be 100% sure if you really do everything in your power to keep it that way.

I don't mean to be iron feast, and you must appreciate the hard work they do for you, and should mention often that you are very happy with the factory. And when your business is going very well, you should show your face by visiting the factory workers. You can also take the factory manager out for a dinner, if you can afford it at least once a year.

Back to documentation, as that's one of the key things that you must practice at all times.

At first if you really want to make sure that everything goes well, you must have a plan for your first large order in regards to quality check. There are many suppliers that when they send out one or two samples they will make sure that it is very well presented. However, once you move on a high volume production you can experience faulty products, and it's vital to have a written plan in order to avoid conflicts that could happen.

There are multiple ways to achieve this; some might cost you lots, like hiring a third party inspection company. However, you might ask your suppliers to carry out self-inspections before shipping.

There is an excellent technique that I used at first, and even since then, and it's completely free. What you do is that you ask your supplier to provide pictures at each phase of the production.

1st Picture:

Once the product comes off the production line and still with no logo on it; It must be the right measurements as well as colours.

2nd Picture:

Once the product has been created, and your logo is visible on it. You might also order an English user guide that also has your logo on it, which you might also want to see and confirm before shipping.

3rd Picture:

The product already in your OEM packaging.

4th Picture:

Once all products are in the box that will be shipped, while the box is still open

5th Picture:

Photo of the Box/Boxes that are now ready to be shipped, clearly visible with the shipping label.

All the above mentioned must be confirmed before placing the order and must be written on the Sales Agreement / Purchasing Agreement.

The reason is that you have to understand that mistakes can be made by your supplier, and it's your responsibility to spot them as early as possible in order to minimize your cost.

An example here is you spot a fault when it comes off the production line, when there is no logo on the product, it will cost lot less to the factory to improve it. However, once they do the screen printing on all 100, or more units, that will be more cost to them and more delay to you.

Stage 2, once there is logo on the product, and you might spot that the logo is not positioned the way you want, or they have used the wrong colour, you must tell them that right then. And you should proceed the same way in regards to the packaging, as well as with the user guide in case you will have that.

Let's say that your products are already shipped to you, and you receive it with all above mentioned faults, you might choose to send it back, but that will cost you so much, and probably your suppliers will not take it back anyways... Or try to sell it that way at a cheaper price, hoping someone will buy the faulty products, or you might as well just bin them.

The worse that can happen is that you didn't spot any of the faults but customers receiving the products did. This can be very bad for your reputation and you will have difficulties creating a good name for your brand.

I hope all that makes sense. Also realize there are plenty of tasks to do, but believe me all this little steps matter in order to be successful, especially if you want to sell your products on Amazon.

Chapter 19 Instagram / Facebook Hacks

Instagram

Instagram is a social media platform where not only can you upload your pictures and very short videos that you personally took, but also edit them with various filters and borders, among other things. Even better, you can post on Instagram and share the same posts on 4 other social media platforms, including Facebook and Twitter, at the same time. Many businesses have started to shift to Instagram marketing for selling their products and services, simply because our minds tend to process information through sight (visuals) and sounds better. Some of the biggest names in the business that are actively marketing their brands on Instagram include Red Bull, Virgin America, Adidas, and Intel. And they do so in different ways.

Virgin America takes a less creative but nevertheless effective approach to marketing on Instagram. An example of this is how they promoted their first-class flights. They simply took photos of the immensely popular Pomeranian puppy named Boo on their flights and posted them on Virgin America's Instagram account.

Others, like Intel, take a relatively more creative approach to Instagram marketing. They market their latest computer processors not by showing pictures of the chips or processors themselves, which are very dull and boring to look at, but by posting well-edited pictures of the top computers that use those processors. By showing off the sexy computers that use the boring-looking chips, Intel is able to engage its audiences and promote their products more effectively by showing on which of the top and visually stimulating computer models their chips are being used in.

The credit card company American Express also takes a creative and indirect approach to promote its credit card services through Instagram. In particular, they don't post pictures of their credit cards - boring and very limited - but instead, post pictures of the activities and events that the company sponsors or has sponsored. They also make use of hashtags on their Instagram posts to position their financial services as being a necessary part of a fulfilling and modern lifestyle.

While you can upload short videos on Instagram, they'll be too short (maximum of 30 seconds only) to be meaningful. If you'd like to upload videos, better do so on YouTube instead. Instagram - for social media marketing purposes - is best suited for posting and editing great pictures.

And speaking of focusing on pictures, social media marketing on this platform isn't as simple as pointing, shooting, and uploading. It's a bit more complicated than that but not so complex that you won't be able to do it yourself. You have to strategically think about and choose the kinds of images you'll share on your brand's Instagram account.

After taking the pictures or images you determined will be best for your social media marketing campaign, you'll need to edit them to give them the most "oomph" and "wow" factor possible. You can edit them on the app itself, right before you post them. Instagram features several cool preset filters or you can customize them yourself using the app if you're familiar with photo-editing concepts. Doing this can turn "ok" into "great" and "ho-hum" into "wow"!

And lastly, you can optimize your image's contribution to your brand's overall social media campaign by coming up with really good hashtags. Doing so can help your images be easily categorized by leading search engines into specific keyword categories, and make them even easier to discover by others.

Other Instagram Best Practices

One specific way to do this on Instagram is to post images or pictures of the people that make up your brand or products and services. And that includes posting pictures of you! Doing so will give your brand a "human" face and something to personally connect to. And when people see the faces behind the brand or product, they're more likely to trust it, engage with it, and patronize it.

Another way to help your prospects and existing customers connect with your brand on a deeper level is to post images and pictures of behind-the-scenes stuff, like how your products are made and packaged, or how it looks like when you render the service you're marketing. Posting pics and images of things like this can help people trust your brand better due to a better sense of familiarity, i.e., they know what goes into your products, who the people rendering your services are, etc. Just be careful not to show too much info on the pics and images so that your competitors won't be able to copy you.

Because Facebook is the Goliath, the Leviathan, and the Paul Bundy of all social media platforms, there's no way you can lose when you promote your brand on these social media platforms. By the sheer volume of prospects alone, it's already worth the effort. But as your favorite infomercials would often say - but wait, there's more!

One of the biggest benefits of marketing on Facebook, especially through paid advertising, is the ability to target your market very specifically. How's that? You see, Facebook isn't just a vast social media platform. It's also probably one of the world's biggest, if not the biggest, database of personal information of billions of people all over the world! You may not be aware of it, but Facebook keeps track of your activities on the platform such as the things you liked, shared, FB accounts or pages followed, where you accessed your account, and so much more. Through such information, Facebook is able to profile you - and everyone else who uses it - with a high degree of accuracy. So Facebook knows who to shoot your content to according to your demographic specifications like age, gender, location, interests, etc.

You can take advantage of Facebook's vast membership, i.e., target market in 2 ways: free content and paid advertising. With free content, you'll have to build your brand's base of followers gradually over time. If you're looking for a longer-term and more economical option, this is your thing. But if you'd like to kick-start your brand's social media marketing and reach a whole lot of people immediately, paid Facebook advertising is the key.

With traditional advertising on print media, TV, or radio, you won't be able to specifically target your desired audience. It's because such forms of advertising are using what's known as a "shotgun" approach, meaning advertisements are thrown at masses of people without concern as to whether or not the right people will see it. That's why traditional advertising is also called mass media advertising. If it happens that most of the people who bought today's paper where you advertised your brand's product or service aren't your target customers or prospects, your advertising money would just go down the drain. Also, mass media advertising is expensive.

Advertising on Facebook is the total opposite of mass media marketing, though it can still reach a big mass of people. First, you have the ability to narrow down the people who would see your advertisement according to many categories such as age, gender, interests, and city among others. So unlike the shotgun approach employed by traditional mass media advertisements, you won't waste your advertising money on prospects that have no chance in hell of buying your products or availing of your services.

Another benefit of using paid Facebook marketing or advertising instead of traditional or mass media advertising is cost. For one, you have complete control over your budget on Facebook ads. You're not forced to toe the line of the advertising rates of traditional mass media outlets, but instead, you can set your own limit on advertising expenses on the platform. And even cooler is the fact that you can also allocate that budget across a specific time period. For example, you can set a budget of $70 for an advertising campaign that will run for 1 week, where Facebook will use up only $10 dollars of your budget daily for the next 7 days. Talk about the ability to control your advertising expenses, eh?

Facebook Marketing

To make the most out of your brand's Facebook marketing, be it paid or free, you must be aware of how things work on Facebook, particularly the platform's marketing practices. Don't think of these as ironclad regulations, but more like signposts or guidelines that can help you optimize your brand's Facebook engagements and conversions en route to higher sales.

Engage

The first thing to keep in mind is the primary goal of social media marketing, which is engagement. If you find it hard to remember most of the guidelines, then at least never forget that engagement is what it's about. Doing so will help you keep the other guidelines in mind.

Okay, going back to engagement, I want you to look at your favorite Facebook pages, whether it's those of your favorite celebrities or brands. Go ahead, put this book down and take a look - and observe. What do you see? That's right...they hardly ever sell directly! What they're doing is engaging you because they know that the higher their level of engagement is with you and all their other followers, the higher the chances of you buying something they're selling or promoting. Why? You don't feel like they're just interested in making you part with your hard-earned money. They make you feel you're an actual person!

So, when "selling" on Facebook, don't "sell" but engage.

If you want to really engage people, the best way to do so is to think as they do. By putting yourself in their position and thinking about what helpful or interesting content you can post on your brand's Facebook page and on its advertisements on the social media platform that they'll like and share. By focusing first on what your target market or audience wants and needs, you'll be able to connect with them, and even develop a relationship. Sales will just be a byproduct of those relationships. Remember, social media marketing is primarily an indirect form of marketing. Right!

Consistency

Another way in which you can effectively market your products and services on Facebook is through content posting consistency. What does this mean?

First, consistency refers to frequency. If you post once a month, your brand will eventually drift out of the consciousness of your audience members, i.e., your prospects and customers, because of the deluge of posts they're exposed to on a daily basis. Posting too frequently can also backfire, i.e., posting twice or thrice daily. So how frequently should you post on your brand's Facebook page?

While there's no hard and fast rule about it, studies have discovered that 3 to 5 times weekly is optimal in many cases, though it may be slightly different according to your brand's unique audience and circumstances. Consider 3 to 5 times weekly as a good starting point and adjust accordingly when needed as you go along.

Consistency also means being consistent with the quality of the content you post on your brand's Facebook page or advertisements. Don't post just for the sake of posting content - make sure whatever you post is of good quality and has a high potential for engagement. Remember that in social media, content is king.

The best way for you to ensure that you always post high-quality and engaging content is to think ahead - plan your brand's

Facebook and other social media platform content in advance. That way, you have enough time to curate excellent content and the opportunity to see how all your content fits together to optimize engagement.

Chapter 20 Is Amazon FBA the Right Service for Me?

If you have a passion for buying and selling, the yes, Amazon FBA is the ideal business platform to consider. After all, since you already love online retail anyway, why not take it a step further and try to make some money out of it? With FBA, what you are doing is scouring for items (shopping) and then reselling them to other customers. Amazon has already made the job easier for you by taking away the worry about storage space, sales, shipping and customer support. All you need to do is find the products you are passionate about selling and get started.

Here is how you can tell whether Amazon FBA is the perfect online business and passive income stream for you:

- You are looking for a long-term side hustle that is dependable.

- You are looking for extra income aside from your regular 9-5 job.

- You want an additional way of making money online, but from the comfort of your home.

- You have always wanted to dabble in entrepreneurship without taking too much risk that is going to land you in debt.

In addition, Amazon FBA is not going to be the perfect business model for you if:

- You are hoping this is going to be a shortcut to getting rich quickly (no such shortcut like that exists, unfortunately).

- You are hoping to make massive profits in a short amount of time.

- You are looking for a quick return on the investment that you put in.

- You do not have the time to commit to doing the necessary work.

Quick Stats and Facts about Amazon's FBA Service

For those who are new to the Amazon FBA scene, here are some quick and important facts that you should keep abreast of. One, more than one Amazon marketplace exists and it depends on where your customers are located. A customer's location is going to determine which Amazon.com store they see. The location will also determine which fulfillment service your customers experience.

Picture 2

By far, Amazon's largest marketplace is none other than the United States of course, which also happens to be the most active marketplace compared to the rest. Amazon's marketplaces are divided into the following categories:

In North America, the marketplaces are:

- *Canada*
- *Mexico*

- United States

In Europe:

- *Spain*
- *Germany*

- United Kingdom

- *France*
- *Italy*

In Asia:

- *India*
- *China*
- *Japan*

Each marketplace's website address will reflect its location. Amazon in the UK, for example, is accessed via Amazon.co.uk. In France, the address would be Amazon.fr, in Japan it's Amazon.co.jp and so on. The location of each marketplace would determine the specific regulations and tax laws, which apply locally depending on the country and region, which you would need to familiarize yourself with before you set up your FBA business.

By default, for most sellers based in the U.S., the marketplace would, of course, be Amazon.com. However, sellers do have the option of branching out and diversifying their products into other regions if they wanted to. The advantage of doing that is you are expanding your services and potentially boosting revenue, but the downside is you might have to deal with higher costs when it comes to shipping. You will also need to have the time to commit to managing different stores in different regions. If you cannot, you will need to have the necessary funds to hire help in managing and operating your multiple stores.

Now, if you are happy just with running a simple retail store with no plans for expansion, then you will not need an e-Commerce website to sell on FBA. However, if you want to take your business a step further, then an e-Commerce store is the way to do. That decision would depend entirely on what your business goals are. One advantage of having an e-Commerce store operating outside Amazon is the opportunity to increase the visibility of your business and products, which means you are increasing your chances of selling more.

Several other reasons to consider an e-Commerce store include:

- More options to explore selling your products other than what is offered by Amazon.

- You get to implement various other strategies to scale your business.

- Opportunity to build on brand equity.

- Opportunity to increase your market reach through advertising.

- Opportunity to build a solid customer base.

- Opportunity to build an email list.

- Opportunity to generate B2B sales

- Better flexibility with products if it is your own website.

Benefits of Using Amazon as a Selling Platform

For an online business to be deemed a success, it needs to be efficient and fast when it comes to shipping (among other things). Amazon has already perfected this aspect into an unbeatable process, going the extra mile to ensure that their shipping is always top-notch. They have been doing this ever since Amazon first went live and they have only improved on their shipping service over time. A large part of why customers keep coming back to Amazon is because of their renowned ability to get their orders to customers in the fastest time possible, no matter where in the world the customer may be.

Among the primary reasons sellers want to do business on Amazon's platform is because when you sell on Amazon, you automatically open up to a huge customer base with a high conversion rate. This is something you are not going to be able to replicate on any other e-commerce platform, eBay included. You are able to make more money by doing less work than you normally would on other platforms. Amazon also offers significant advantages, especially for sellers seeking to reach a large and diverse clientele that is ready to spend money online, in a short amount of time.

Amazon has - and always will - put their customers first above anything. The company continues to strive to create better shopping experiences; even going so far as to try to improve their shipping times so they can deliver products even faster than what they are already doing. It also continues to work hard to improve the overall shopping experience customers get when they come to their website. When you sell on Amazon, you are selling with the best of the best. The other benefits you stand to gain include:

- *A Willing and Ready Customer Base* - Amazon's power lies in its large customer base, all of whom are ready and willing to purchase products that they need. By selling on Amazon, compared to many other retail platforms, the number of potential customers is more than triple the number of potential customers on eBay. This means you have an incredible opportunity in your hands. The chance to reach an ever-ready crowd, ready to buy online the minute they set up their business using Amazon. Sellers on Amazon can reach 237 million customers.

- *Customer Spending Power* - Customers love retail shopping. More importantly, they love retail shopping on Amazon more than any other platform. Amazon's revenue in June 2018 surged to $81.76 billion. Consequently, eBay reported $17.05 billion in that same period. An RBC survey even revealed that the average customer who shops on Amazon would spend approximately $320 annually. These numbers are very promising from a seller's point of view. It is an opportunity for sellers to gain depth and breadth where the visibility of their business is concerned.

- *Its Undisputed Reputation* - Amazon has a credible reputation. When it comes to credibility, no other platform can hold a candle to Amazon, thanks to its exceptional customer service and shipping. This has enabled Amazon to hold a large market share of online consumers simply because of their amazing services. This is something to keep in mind if you are deciding between eBay and Amazon.

- *The Power of Prime* - Amazon Prime can absolutely increase your revenues and increase the number of customers. With Prime, Amazon encourages customers to spend a little bit more by giving incentives such as two-day free shipping on plenty of Prime products. Prime customers spent an average of $528 a year compared to $320 spent by non-Prime Amazon customers.

- *Absence of Listing Fees* - While some platforms charge fees just to list products, Amazon does not. You will only be charged when you have made a sale. As a seller, this means you can list as many items as you would like on Amazon and then leave them until a customer has purchased them. The slight downside with this one is, the sales fee is rather hefty, with Amazon taking at least 20% of the profit. This fee is even higher if you are an FBA seller but of course, when you become an FBA seller, you are doing less work, therefore it balances out in the end.

- *No Relisting Needed* - A huge, hassle-free advantage that Amazon has over platforms like eBay is there is no need to continuously relist your items the way you would need to on eBay. Unless you sign up for the FBA service though, you are going to have to handle the shipping and customer service aspect of the business yourself.

- *You Can Charge Slightly Higher Prices* - Customers would be willing to pay the extra too, for the sake of the guarantee that comes with Amazon. Amazon, at the end of the day, is an online retailer. Like other retailers, they make their money by selling items at competitive rates. This process contrasts with that of a wholesaler, who charges you the lowest possible price, especially if you buy in bulk. eBay acts as a wholesale market and charges the lowest price. For example, a t-shirt may cost $15 on eBay but on Amazon, the same t-shirt might cost you $20. The reason for this increase is that Amazon sells new items (although there are used options available for certain products too), whereas eBay sells mostly used items.

- *Home of Reliable Brands* - Amazon stocks some of the most reliable brands on the market. As one of the most trusted retail names out there, Amazon and many of its customers are willing to pay $99 a year to be part of the Prime service. If you sell your products through Amazon, your business is then associated with a trusted brand. If you are a budding brand or the average online entrepreneur trying to make ends meet, Amazon is a good starting point. You get to access their large customer base while you learn the ropes of the business, before expanding to sell your products on shelves like Walmart.

- *An Excellent Learning Platform* - Business is a risk, but you can minimize that risk when you sell on Amazon. You can use the Amazon platform to test your target market for the products you plan to sell. By selling on Amazon, you gain access to retail data that enables you to see how your product is doing, what the demand is and what you can charge for your product.

- *Driving Awareness* - Amazon can be a great tool used to drive traffic to your other websites. Even better if you have a social media account or blog. It can be a valuable source of buyer information, which can give you great input on how to sell your products from what offers customers like, what they do not like, best times to open for promotions and so on. This should be part of your marketing strategy, to plan for long-term and sustainable success.

- *Perks of Amazon Associates* - You can take advantage of Amazon Associates services to market and promote products related to the industry on your website. Amazon Associates is an affiliate program that allows sellers to earn commissions through affiliate links. A slight downside with this option here is that there will be a clash of interest on the products you sell and the ones you promote. One way to avoid this conflict is by selecting products you promote meticulously and not burn your business.

- *Getting A Boost in Sales of 30-50%* - This boost primarily comes from Amazon's Prime program. Many shoppers do not like the idea of having to pay for shipping and Prime and stepped up to solve that problem. As a Prime user, you are entitled to 2-days of free shipping on any Prime-eligible products. This, in turn, increases the shopper's probability of purchases. Combine that with the "trust factor", where Amazon has built an undisputed reputation for itself and your sales are going to jump exponentially. When a customer sees the "Shipped by Amazon" or "Fulfilled by Amazon" indicator, there is a sense of relief and peace of mind. They know their products are safe and they are not going to be scammed, which is a very real probability if they were to purchase from an unknown merchant with no long-standing history.

- *You do not have to worry about Shipping* - You would be surprised at how tedious and time consuming the shipping and handling process can be. Once again, it is a huge relief for merchants, knowing that Amazon is going to take care of all of that for them. Amazon is the expert when it comes to shipping and they have gone to great lengths to ensure continued quality service, in the fastest and most reliable way. This gives FBA sellers a wonderful and must-not-miss opportunity to capitalize on that. Sellers get to save a lot of time and resources, which they would otherwise have to divert towards handling the shipping aspect. With that out of the way, you are left free and clear to focus entirely on advertising and marketing your products.

- *You Gain the Trust of Your Customers* - With products guaranteed to arrive, customers will love any business running under Amazon and its FBA label. It is not only Americans that love and trust Amazon either. Customers around the world have been turning to the retail giant for years to have their needs met. It is irrefutable what those three simple words *"Fulfilled by Amazon"* can do for your sales figures. Even if the customer has never heard of you until you, they will be completely comfortable purchasing from you, thanks again to the level of trust that is associated with Amazon. Shoppers are more likely to purchase from a retailer they know without a doubt that they can trust.

- *You are Automatically Eligible for Prime* - With 64% of American households being members of Amazon Prime that is almost 85 million customers who are currently using this premier service. Those who are members of Prime are *not* going to buy products that are not eligible for the Prime option. Having that Prime logo is tapping into the trust factor once again and when it comes to selling on Amazon FBA, Prime is definitely the way to go.

- *You Get Access to the "Buy Box"* - Amazon's "buy box" is the white box, which is located on the right, the same section where customers can click on the "Add to Cart" or "Buy Now" options. If you are wondering why this box matters so much, here is why. On Amazon, you will find two types of sellers. One is Amazon themselves; the second is third party. The latter category is made up of every company who is *not a part* of Amazon themselves. If you have your own eCommerce store, this is you. Now, several of these third-party businesses are going to be selling the same product, with the same details listed on their site. The sellers then, compete to win the "Buy Box", because, with this option on your page, you become the seller whose product is selected. Your product becomes the one customers add to their cart or buy now. 83% of sales on Amazon happen through the Buy Box option, which makes it a statistic you cannot ignore. In addition, yes, you have to "win" this option and it is Amazon who determines who the winner is. Amazon relies on an algorithm, which then determines the seller who will be represented in the Buy Box and for what duration. One thing's for sure, the Buy Box is going to give you a lot of preference as an FBA seller.

Chapter 21 Mistakes to Avoid

Not creating expandable brands and product lines from the start: If you are planning to build a sustainable business brand, you will want a larger umbrella of products to expand your business in the long run. Pick primary products that have plenty of complimentary purchases or can be bundled together with other items. This way you can keep adding items to create a longer product line under your brand. For example, if you zero in on the electronic gadgets niche, you may have a whole bunch of accessories and replaceable parts to sell to under a single business brand.

Go with bundled products and multi-packs if you are looking to score really big with Amazon FBA. Single items that sell are unlikely to be competition free or low competition on Amazon. Almost all products that sell reasonably well have tons of merchants in the category. Also, profit on one item products is swallowed by Amazon fees. Unless you can find a sweet spot between a high priced product that is also in demand and has low competition, you may not be able to achieve stellar results with single items.

Also, your woes will increase if Amazon sells the product. Unless you have a terrific edge, it is going to be hard to compete with Amazon. Bundling up products or creating multi-packs may require greater time or money. You need to source a variety of items and bundle them. However, it can be highly beneficial for long term profits.

Underestimating the holidays: As long as you are comfortable holding on to these items for roughly 10 months, the deals you can find on decorations during the days immediately after most major holidays can practically guarantee acceptable profit margins on nearly everything you can imagine. What's more, by waiting 10 months before sending them to Amazon, you minimize your storage costs while at the same time taking advantage of all the people who like to plan for the holidays early. Alternately, you can wait until just a few weeks prior to the holiday to post your products and raise the prices even more to grab customers who waited until the last second and as a result, don't care about the costs.

Another good place to look is in the autocomplete results of search engines on websites like eBay or Etsy, places where people are already going to search for harder to find items. In fact, if you ultimately find that the community for buying and selling related items is particularly robust, you may wish to consider starting a store on one of these platforms yourself.

Not listing products the right way

Even though we are told time and time again not to judge a book by its cover, shopping on Amazon, and anywhere online in general, is quite the opposite. One of the vital aspects of any listing on Amazon is the title, which informs potential buyers what the product is all about.

- Add keywords to the title to help the product to rank when buyers search

- Incorporate brand name

- Incorporate the name of the product
Add any features that distinguish the item

  - Its use

  - Color

  - Size

For instance, if you are selling a pacifier, an ideal title would look something similar to this: Deluxe Silicone Baby Pacifier – Easy for Parents – BPA Free – Set of 2 Pacifiers – Blue

Goals for an Amazon product title should do the following:

  - Educate potential consumers about the product, even before they read the product page

  - Add a few keywords to showcase the product and its use

Not taking full advantage of images: Another important aspect of the product details of items on Amazon is the images included in the listing. They can cause shoppers to click on your listing just because of the quality of the image. That's why you should spend a good amount of time to research images that are top-notch. Amazon product images should include:

- Showcase product size by having a human hold it

- Information images like charts

- Images that include features of the product and compare it to other similar items

- Images of your product being utilized

  - The back label

- The item from all different angles

A great resource to find top-notch Amazon images for your listings that are also affordable is AMZDream.com.

Not using enough bullet points: If potential buyers fail to be swooned by your choice of title and images, bullet points are the next best thing to get a straightforward reaction. You have five spaces to include bullet points, but this doesn't mean you only have to use five words or even sentences. I personally use short paragraphs in each of those bullet points to home in on benefits and features of the item. Address common questions and objections as well. Use the first three points to showcase your products most pertinent features and use the other bullet points to answer common inquiries or customer objections.

Not pricing products properly: Opt to sell private label products that are priced above $10. Amazon lists items priced below $10 as "Add On Items, which means buyers cannot purchase your item by itself. They have to make additional purchases to be able to buy your product. Additionally, profit margins for products priced below $10 after deducting Amazon's fee can be rather low for building a lucrative, long-term business. You will need a very higher sales volume to witness recent returns. Ideally, pick products that sell in the range of $10-$30 for higher profit margins.

Few things will kill you like low cost products on Amazon unless you predict an unrealistically high sales volume. You may think inexpensive items carry less risk or are more frequently picked up by customers on impulse. However, selling products for below $5 is not likely to be profitable even with a high sales volume or next to nothing sourcing price. The shipping cost (to Amazon's warehouse) and fees will leave you with a few pennies.

Not treating it like a business: While Amazon FBA is not the same as having your traditional website up and running where you sell products to people, you should still treat the time that you spend on Amazon FBA the same that you would like an e-commerce business. Even though using Amazon FBA allows you to move away from creating your website, this does not mean that you should not take Amazon FBA seriously. You can lose money through this platform if you're not accurate in your estimates or you're sloppy with your profit margin calculations.

Not doing enough research: Another tip that many Amazon FBA users miss is that they don't do research on the Amazon site itself before deciding which products they're going to sell. Even if you enjoy fishing, this does not necessarily mean that selling fishing poles on Amazon is a decision that is going to lead to profits. Look at what's selling the most frequently on Amazon, and take note of any markets that may look like they're being underrepresented.

Having too many similar products: Unlike the notion of a niche website that we've already discussed, you do not have to worry about keeping a product line that is similar when you're using Amazon FBA. Because your seller profile is not going to define the type of business that you're running, you have the freedom to pick and choose the products that you want to sell. This can be great for someone who is good at doing research on products within Amazon's website. By figuring out the profit margin that's possible from certain products that are on the market, you should be able to make better financial decisions for yourself and your business.

Chapter 22 Frequently Asked Questions

What does Fulfillment by Amazon represent?

Fulfillment by Amazon (FBA) is a very interesting option provided by this platform, which can help merchants boost their business by taking advantage of Amazon's expertise and resources, fast, free and trustworthy shipment, and outstanding customer support services. By choosing this option, you can send your inventory to the platform's warehouses (fulfillment centers) so that they can be stored over there and then leave everything to Amazon, including the picking, packing, and shipping of your customers' orders.

FBA is eligible for all the product categories and subcategories showing up on the Amazon Seller account. It is also available for any reseller who is curious to try it. The maximum weight limit for this program is 30 kilograms per product, so this is a requirement you need to know right from the start. You can test how your products are selling on Amazon, as well as send plenty of them to the fulfillment centers because you don't have to pay for anything upfront. You merely have to spend on their services that you use at the end of the month or when you make a sale.

What exactly is the Amazon Seller Central?

When selecting the selling plan, you should be able to see the prices of both plans easily. The Individual account costs $0.99, while the Professional one amounts to $39.99. These are both monthly fees, and you are charged 30 days after the registration process.

Is it possible to create an Amazon Selling account for free?

Unfortunately, this is not an option on this platform because you need to choose between an Individual or Professional account.

What do I have to do in order to comply with Amazon's return policy?

Amazon will ask you to provide the following methods for returns:

- a return address;
- a prepaid return level; and
- a full refund without asking for the product to be returned.

How do consumers recognize the Fulfillment by Amazon products on the platform?

These products have the "Fulfillment by Amazon" logo, which provides the customers with the information that support service, returns, packing, and delivery are handled by Amazon.

How to label individual products?

When you wish to add your listings on the platform, you will be faced with a decision that can influence your further success on Amazon. To be precise, you have to select the labelling option, whether you want to send the products using EAN or UPC barcodes (these products fall into the Commingled Inventory or Stickerless category), or label the products properly (Labeled Inventory) to hide the original barcode completely. Commingled Inventory can be combined with other inventories from different merchants; that's why your customers might get products from different resellers, which may or may not have the same features as yours. Amazon will not open the boxes to check which product is the right one and from which merchant it has come from to ensure the authenticity of the merchandise. The Stickerless option, on the other hand, only refers to the products, not to the delivery. Although it may be a bit time-consuming and complicated, you may need to label the items well to protect your inventory and make sure that your customers are getting what they have ordered.

How to print labels for your own products?

When you are adding new products (inventory) from your Seller Central account (you will need to go into "Inventory Amazon Fulfils" and then "Send/replenish inventory") or just preparing an inventory, you are entering something called "shipping workflow." It will provide extra guidance on how to prepare your inventory to be shipped to Amazon's warehouses, thus giving you the option to customize the shipment considering the selections that you make during each step. At one point, you will be prompted to choose the labelling option and allow you to print your unit labels from the shipping workflow directly. These tags will include details like the product title, which can prove to be very helpful when it comes to matching the label with the right product. You need a printer and blank adhesive papers to print such labels, which can be found on the Amazon website or any store that sells office supplies.

Is there a possibility for Amazon to add the labels on your products?

This is a possible option, especially when you are entering the shipping workflow guide. You can simply select Amazon Label Service when prompted with the labelling options. This is a valid solution if you find the private label process too complicated and time-consuming.

How to pack products when sending them to Amazon?

You can find two different types of packing products before sending them to Amazon's warehouses below.

- Individually packed goods means that every box contains one or few units, depending on conditions and quantities.
- Packing items in a case is an option that will allow the merchant to place the products with the same SKU and

condition into one box. The boxes will have the same quantity and the same item in them. When Amazon receives these boxes, they will only scan one item from the box and place the whole thing in your inventory. Amazon does not need to scan all the items, considering they are all the same.

When the reseller sends the products to Amazon, they can only be sent using one type of packing per shipment. Although they will be added to the inventory, if the merchant has individually packed items and cases with packed items, he or she will need to send them separately to Amazon.

How to choose a shipping method and carrier to send your inventory to Amazon?

The starting point of creating a new shipment is the "Send/replenish inventory" tab, which is present in the "Inventory Amazon Fulfils" section of your account. It is also possible when you have a work-in-progress inventory and you use the "shipping workflow" tool. By using the latter, you will receive step-by-step instructions on how to prepare your merchandise to be sent over to Amazon, including details about customizing your shipment according to the selections that you make at each step. One of them will allow you to choose from the shipping methods below:

- Small Parcel Deliveries (SPDs) represent individually packed and labelled products (one product per box), all prepared to be shipped.
- Less-Than-Truckload (LTL) shipments are, in fact, a mixed delivery because it contains pallets and individually boxed products. In this case, some of the products may be sent to different destinations, different warehouses.
- Full Truckload (FTL) also combines full pallets and individually packed products. The difference, however, is that the whole merchandise is going to one warehouse.

The FBA terms and conditions apply to all products that you send to and are meant to be sold on Amazon, regardless of the shipping method that you select. You can find more details related to how the platform receives and routes your products if you check these terms and conditions.

You can also choose a different carrier, other than the one provided by Amazon. Costs can be higher in this case, but if you do want to go ahead with this option, you will need to work with a trusted carrier that is capable of providing you with valuable information like a valid tracking number for SPD, the pro/freight bill number for FTL or LTL deliveries, and the bill of lading (BOL).

You can't send the inventory to Amazon using a privately-owned car, however. It can only be done by a registered carrier.

How to create shipping labels?

The shipping workflow is a sequence and tool where you can simply choose the type of labels that you want to have (if there is any). When selecting Small Parcel Delivery (SPD), you will be prompted to print shipping labels (just one per box) and packing slips. You will also need to place the packing slip inside the box, on the top side, so that it can be seen immediately after being opened at the Amazon's warehouse. The information that you should include are the destination and return addresses, while the label should be positioned just outside the sealed box as an addition to labels added by the carrier.

If you select Less-Than-Truckload, you still need to print a label per each box, which has to be placed outside of it so it can be seen when unwrapping the pallet. On the pallets, the tags have to be placed in a top-center position on each side (on the stretched wrap).

Adhesive labels can be found at any office supplies store or on Amazon.

Is it possible to arrange a shipment of inventory directly from an overseas supplier?

This is not an acceptable option because Amazon can't be used as the final address, importer or consignee when sending products from overseas. In this case, merchants will have to make the necessary arrangement to import and clear the shipment of customs. Only after doing this that they can send the inventory to Amazon's warehouses.

How to notify Amazon in advance regarding the products that I'm sending to them?

You have three options of sending products over to Amazon: Small Parcel Delivery (SPD), Less-Than-Truckload (LTL), and Full Truckload (FTL). For the last two choices, you will need to arrange delivery appointments; otherwise, the fulfillment centers may decline your shipment. In order to arrange a delivery appointment with the warehouse where you want to send the inventory, you will need first to download the Fulfillment by Amazon booking form, fill it, and email it to the carrier. In this form, you will have to place the ZIP code (you can find it in the Shipping Queue section of your account). Once the carrier has received your form, they will send it to the Amazon's Fulfillment Center to schedule the best delivery timing. It usually takes around 24 hours for the warehouse to reply back to the carrier with a confirmation for the delivery time.

Conclusion

After reading through this guide, you should feel informed and ready to get started embarking on the journey of FBA business ownership. The benefits are obvious and the potential for profit is enormous if you are willing to put in the strategic work and effort. Many people have invested the time and turned Amazon into their main source of income – now you can too.

It starts off simply: creating your account and arming yourself with the tools of the trade. With the right apps, you can figure out the best way to get a bang for your buck. You'll become an expert at the practice of buying low and selling high, especially with the help of the tools that software developers are continually improving.

Once you've built up your inventory of items you sought out with expertise for their appropriate ranking and adherence to Amazon restrictions and guidelines, you are ready to start a shipment. The packing materials are costly, but remember that you will be able to deduct the cost from your income at the end of the tax season. When you create a shipment with your Amazon Seller account, you will receive detailed instructions on how to pack your shipment and where to send it.

When you've sent your first shipment, be aware of the selling and storage fees that will be levied against you. The advantages of being a professional seller are numerous, but particularly with regard to these selling fees, since you won't pay extra for every item. Use the FBA revenue calculator, another tool in your toolbox, to determine the potential earnings from your sale.

If you feel comfortable with retail arbitrage but are seeking to take it to the next level, or if you are entering Amazon FBA with previous experience selling online, private labeling is for you. Buying inventory cheaply and marketing it under your personal brand is a way to ramp up your earnings. The competition is fierce, but if you choose your products wisely, it can have huge rewards. Even with the right product choice, you will still need to do the most to market your business and get the coveted Buy Box benefits.

A lot of marketing is just common sense: you need to have an attractive sales page so your products present well. There are tricks of the trade, however, that will improve your standing. Offering discounts can help get you the necessary exposure to generate reviews, and taking advantage of Amazon's advertising function with the help of keyword-finding aids will improve your chances – as long as you know how to properly invest in your campaigns.

The technical side of things can get complicated, but this guide should help you feel more comfortable in the awareness of the potential pitfalls that lie ahead. Amazon businesses are rewarding, but you need to be properly equipped with the right legal knowledge in order to avoid the consequences of a mismanaged business.

Once you get started with Amazon FBA, you may find yourself encountering unique issues that aren't addressed in this guide. For those situations, you can address your inquiry to the online community of the FBA Sellers through Seller Central or on other communities like Reddit. There forums offer a framework for the exchange of novel ideas that could revolutionize your selling. Be open to the suggestions of others, as they could help you get ahead of the game.

Lastly, never fail to remember the importance of investing in yourself, for yourself. With Amazon FBA, you are in control. This means you have to be capable of motivating yourself to make the most of this opportunity. The more work you are willing to put into FBA, the more you will get out of it, but only if you are willing to go the distance. It may be called passive income, but you have to actively strive to reach that point. The time you don't spend going after your share of the market is time you leave to other people to take it from you. After reading this book, the next step is to go register as an FBA seller. Armed with this knowledge, the success is yours for the taking.

www.ingramcontent.com/pod-product-compliance
Lightning Source LLC
Chambersburg PA
CBHW070348220526
45467CB00001B/293